WAS THERE A
FIFTH MAN?

Quintessential Recollections

Other Titles of Interest

WILFRID MANN is the co-author with R L AYRES and S B GARFINKEL of *Radioactivity and its Measurement*, 2nd Revised and Expanded Edition, Pergamon Press, Oxford, 1980.

WAS THERE A
FIFTH MAN?

Quintessential Recollections

by
WILFRID BASIL MANN

PERGAMON PRESS

Oxford · New York · Toronto · Sydney · Paris · Frankfurt

U.K.	Pergamon Press Ltd., Headington Hill Hall, Oxford OX3 0BW, England
U.S.A.	Pergamon Press Inc., Maxwell House, Fairview Park, Elmsford, New York 10523, U.S.A.
CANADA	Pergamon Press Canada Ltd., Suite 104, 150 Consumers Rd., Willowdale, Ontario M2J 1P9, Canada
AUSTRALIA	Pergamon Press (Aust.) Pty. Ltd., P.O. Box 544, Potts Point, N.S.W. 2011, Australia
FRANCE	Pergamon Press SARL, 24 rue des Ecoles, 75240 Paris, Cedex 05, France
FEDERAL REPUBLIC OF GERMANY	Pergamon Press GmbH, 6242 Kronberg-Taunus, Hammerweg 6, Federal Republic of Germany

First edition 1982

Library of Congress Cataloging in Publication Data
Mann, W. B. (Wilfrid Basil), 1908–
Was there a fifth man?

Includes index.
1. Mann, W. B. (Wilfrid Basil), 1908–
2. Physicists—United States—Biography.
3. Philby, Kim, 1912– . 4. Burgess, Guy Francis de Moncy, 1911–1963. 5. Maclean, Donald Duart, 1913– .
6. Espionage, Russian—Great Britain—History. I. Title.
QC16.M345A38 1981 327.1′2′0924[B] 81–17773
                                                     AACR2

British Library Cataloguing in Publication Data
Mann, Wilfrid B.
Was there a fifth man?
1. Espionage, Russian—Great Britain—History—
20th century
I. Title
327.1′2′09470924   UB271.R9
ISBN 0–08–027445–5

Printed in Great Britain by A. Wheaton & Co. Exeter

Publishers' Note

The author and the publishers wish to thank all those who have generously allowed us to quote from copyrighted sources: The Controller of Her Majesty's Stationery Office for material previously published in *Statements Relating to the Atomic Bomb* (1945); the Editor of *The Sunday Times* for the extract from a review by Phillip Knightley of *The Climate of Treason* by Andrew Boyle, published in June 1980; the Editor of *The Daily Telegraph* for permission to quote from an article by Stephen Barber (November 1979); Penthouse International Limited and *The Times* in respect of the article by Mr Tad Szulc entitled "CIA 'gave technological support to Israel to make an atomic bomb...'" (1975); and to the Editor of *The Washington Post* who granted permission for a maximum of 200 words to be quoted from Allen Weinstein's article "Spy Hunt" published by them in January 1980; to the Head of the Federal Bureau of Investigation for the release of the material which forms the subject of part of Chapter 9; to the publishers of *Fra Fysikkens Verden* (the journal of the Norwegian Physical Society) for the extensive quotation from the author's tribute to Professor Leif Tronstad, published in 1965; and to all those providing photographic material, the credits for which are given in the captions to the plates. Every attempt has been made to trace sources of quotations where it is considered that these may go beyond the convention of "fair dealing", but any copyright holder of unacknowledged material is asked to get in touch with the publishers.

Preface

Reluctantly I am venturing to write a very short account of my professional life in the service, at different times, of each of the three countries that joined forces at the Quebec Conference in 1943 to produce the atom bomb. My profession is that of an experimental physicist, and I have engaged in research in several branches of physics, including that of experimental nuclear physics. It happens too that, while having appeared only once briefly on stage myself, I have often stood in the wings exchanging greetings with the principal actors as they made their entrances and exits.

For reasons that I hope the text will make clear, I have been identified, though always in a way which was just short of actionable, with the so-called "Fifth Man" of the long-running British spy saga. For the sake of my family and myself, I feel that I have a duty to put the record straight before myth has time to trespass on history.

In 1950, when Dean Acheson, then Secretary of State, in company with George Marshall, Secretary of Defense, had his loyalty viciously impugned by Senators William Jenner and Joseph McCarthy, it is said that he "found it difficult to conceal his contempt for the contemptible".* Although contempt may be a very understandable attitude in

---

*Quoted from Douglas Freeman in Dean Acheson's own book *Present at the Creation*, pp 246 and 366 (W W Norton & Company Inc, New York, 1969).

such circumstances, it hardly offers concrete evidence as to the nature of one's deeds, or even thoughts, in every waking moment of one's life. Nor is it easy to *prove* the *non-existence* of some thing or some act, past or present. Thus any one, however innocent, at whom a finger is pointed in the context of spying would have difficulty in producing evidence to the contrary; every minute of his life would have to be scrutinized.*

Attempts have been made to identify me with the "Basil" referred to in a recently published book.† It is impossible for me to prove that this character "Basil" never existed, although, because of my association with many of the same persons, places and events at about that time in history, I am convinced that he did not. I can prove, however, that the "Basil" described was not I, although I believe that the semi-fictional work that first used that cryptonym is but the latest of several attempts to mould such a character in the likeness of my own—that of a "British-born physicist, now an American citizen working for the United States Government in Washington, with special and esoteric ties with the CIA".‡

In the following pages I have made extensive use of dated correspondence and publications to show precisely where I was at the times that "Basil" was supposed to have been operating in collusion with Donald Maclean at the British Embassy in Washington. Copies of these letters have been made available to the publisher of this book, and the scientific publications can be viewed in many libraries. My passports have been examined and the dates therein verified by Mr John de St Jorré and by Professor Allen Weinstein, to both of whom I am very grateful. The misfit between "Basil" and me is epitomized by the fact that when he was supposed to be entering the scene in Washington for an extensive sojourn, I was actually leaving Washington for the United Kingdom.

The many references to letters and to scientific journals in the early chapters of this book may be of interest only to the more sleuth-minded

---

*This precise point was made very clearly by Mrs Margaret Thatcher in the House of Commons on 26 March 1981 when in discussing the allegations of treachery against Sir Roger Hollis, she said that innocence in such a context could never be proved beyond all possible doubt.

†*The Climate of Treason: Five Who Spied for Russia* by Andrew Boyle (Hutchinson, London, 1979).

‡Quoted from *The Times* of 21 August, 1975, and *Penthouse,* September 1975.

of its possible readers. To my mind, however, the post-"Basil" era is more interesting—namely the era that began on my return to Washington in December 1948, the description of which starts in Chapter 5.

In conclusion, I wish to acknowledge with deep appreciation the great help and support that has been extended to me by many friends and colleagues both at home and abroad. In particular the following have provided very substantial assistance and advice in the midst of the circumstances that led to my writing this book, or in discussing or reading parts or all of its text: Ernest Ambler, James Angleton, James Cobban, J J Coyne, Peggy Ducker, Allen Farrar, Richard Franzen, Lloyd and Elsbeth Free, C L Haslam, Matt Heyman, Will Jacobs, Caroline McCoy Jones, Alexander King, W Bennett Lewis, Robert Maxwell, Ian and Patricia Meanock, Phyllis Pierce, William Randolph, Marsha Swiss, Lauriston Taylor, Richard Van Wagenen, Algie Wells, and, not least, my wife Miriam and my family.

There are also those who are no longer here to be thanked, but whose influence in varying degrees on the course of my life I gladly acknowledge: Sir John Cockcroft, Sir Alfred Egerton, Professor A V Hill, Professor Ernest Lawrence, Sir George Thomson and Sir Henry Tizard.

W B Mann
Washington, DC

Contents

List of Illustrations

1

The Family of Mann

I made my début into this world on 4 August 1908, my father's thirtieth birthday. Six years later, on my birthday, Great Britain declared war on Germany. My father volunteered for service in the Royal Flying Corps, but was rejected because of less than perfect eyesight. For the rest of the war I remember that he and my mother kept open house for friendly blue-uniformed wounded soldiers with whom I enjoyed week-end outings in our four-seater open car that rejoiced in the name of "Alldays and Onions" and was my father's pride. I also remember the first Zeppelin raid on London. Then after the war in 1918 my father ran for parliament as a National Party candidate, and narrowly missed being elected, in the constituency of North East Ham.

My paternal grandparents were Irish Catholics who brought up their family of six sons in accordance with the precepts of the Church, although on week-days, from all accounts, the boys led my grandparents a merry chase.

My mother, Maud Mary Cogan, was also Catholic, but only half-Irish. Her father was in general medical practice, having graduated from Trinity College, Dublin, and she took considerable pride in the fact that her grandfather was the squire of Fermoy in southern Ireland. My maternal grandmother was a Staffordshire woman who died while my mother was in her late teens. My mother had two sisters and an only

1

brother, Albert Cogan, who was killed in action in World War I. She met my father in Hammersmith and at the time of my birth they were living in Ealing. It is not surprising, given my parents' background, that my mother should have turned to the Litany of the Saints when choosing names for my sister and for me. It might have been more surprising, however, to that great fourth-century saint, Basil, to know that his name, given to a not very saintly twentieth-century scientist, should subsequently be employed—not perhaps coincidentally—as a code-name in that world of espionage literature where fact and fiction are so hard to discern.

But that is looking forward to the future. Most of my youth was spent in Surrey where my only sister was born in 1913. From 1922 until 1927 I was a day-boy at St Paul's School, which was still in those buildings in West Kensington which were destined to provide a home, twenty years later, for the planning staff of 21st Army Group before the invasion of Europe. It was not until 1968 that the School itself was moved to its present position south of the river.

St Paul's had been founded by Dean Colet in 1509 for the study of "good Latin and Greek". I did my quota of the good Latin and then, on entry to the sixth form (traditionally known at St Paul's at the VIIIth), came the parting of the ways. My choice of the science side for my last two years at school—a choice not as common then as it is now— was influenced by my father's suggestion that I might become a patent lawyer, and at the patent bar a scientific background can be a great advantage. In spite of the fact that my career followed a different pattern, I have never regretted the decision.

Nor do I regret rowing in the 2nd VIII, even though this may have affected my academic achievement. However, I secured a place at the Imperial College of Science and Technology which I entered in 1927 with the help of a leaving Exhibition from St Paul's—thus beginning a connection with the College which continued intermittently until 1946.

Having learned my lesson at St Paul's, I eschewed serious rowing for the first two years at the Imperial College and passed the necessary qualifying examinations at the end of the second year, being awarded the Governor's Prize in Physics for first place. I had, however, to spend a third year on a research project before receiving my bachelor's degree from the University of London. In this third year, by way of compensation, I neglected science, to some extent, in favour of rowing and spent an idyllic summer at Henley and every other regatta on the Thames, very pleasantly but with less than outstanding success. I had won the Imperial College Junior and Senior sculls in 1928 and 1929, respectively (it is a form of rowing which demands less time) and in 1930 I was elected captain of rowing at the Royal College of Science, one of the three constituent colleges of the Imperial College of Science and Technology.

After my final examinations in 1929, that gentle but incisive authority on the properties of steam, Professor Hugh L Callendar, offered me a demonstratorship in physics at the then princely salary of £250 per annum. I recall his making the offer with all but his head and shoulders diffidently hidden by the three-quarter closed door of his office to which he was just returning from his laboratory in the basement. His head was covered as usual by an old cloth cap that was said to protect it from the hot water dripping from the superheated steam pipes of his apparatus. He was a very fine and down-to-earth scientist. A salesman once tried to commend a piece of equipment to him by telling him that it was fool-proof, to which Callendar wisely replied that nothing is fool-proof if you have a big enough fool. Later I was to recall his comment when I was told that certain buildings in Berkeley were earthquake-proof!

Professor Callendar died in 1930 and was succeeded by George Thomson, the son of J J Thomson, the following year. In the meantime Professor A O Rankine asked me to give the lectures previously given by Callendar. In honour of G P Thomson's arrival from Aberdeen, where he had demonstrated the wave nature of the electron by photographing the diffraction patterns arising from the scattering of electrons by crystals, I composed a limerick:

> The electron mass m and charge e
> When diffracted is easy to see.
> The positive ray
> Attracted J.J.
> The electron, diffracted, G. P.

From 1929 to 1931 my fellow graduate, Basil Gordon Dickins, and I researched under the tutelage of Professor H S Gregory into the thermal conductivities of saturated hydrocarbons in the gaseous state. A paper on the subject was prepared for submission to the Royal Society and we solemnly tossed a coin for order of authorship. To our surprise the paper was not only accepted but actually selected for reading and, as I had "won" the toss of the coin, I was faced now with this ordeal. I can still remember the thrill when after the meeting the Secretary, Sir James Jeans, took the trouble to compliment us, in the kindest terms, on our paper.

In the ten years before the War I was lucky enough to have two extended sojourns abroad. The first came when I was awarded a London University Travelling Studentship for the academic year 1932–3, which I decided to spend at Den Polytekniske Laereanstalt (now the Technical University) in Copenhagen. There I worked with that grand old researcher into the kinetic theory of gases, Professor Martin Knudsen. G P Thomson had also given me an introduction to Professor Niels Bohr, by whom Copenhagen, at that time, was being turned into the Mecca of theoretical physics.

Niels Bohr immediately gave me an open invitation to attend all seminars and functions at his Instittutet for Teoretisk Fysik (now the *Niels Bohr* Institute) and also to "drop in" any Saturday afternoon at his home in Gammle Carlsberg for music and tea. I remember two occasions, one at Gammle Carlsberg and one at the Institute, that remain impressed upon my memory after the passing of nearly fifty years. In the first, I was sitting at a table in the winter garden with Fru Bohr, and two or three theoretical physicists, including our good friend Oscar Klein from Stockholm, were competing to see how high they could elevate a ping-pong ball on the single jet of the fountain. The higher the ping-pong ball the greater the hilarity: Fru Bohr turned to me and said "Aren't physicists children?" Unconsciously, she had put her finger on one of the qualities of the physicist—the ability to look at natural phenomena with the direct simplicity of the child. The gardener in the orchard might have made the same remark when he saw good Master Newton gazing so intently at the falling applies.

The second occasion was the opening of the annual conference at the Institute in the spring of 1933. The positive electron had been observed the previous year by C D Anderson thus providing an answer to P A M Dirac's prediction of a short-lived "hole" in a continuum of negative-energy states that would be manifested as a positive particle. Niels Bohr opened the proceedings with an enthusiastic tribute to Dirac, leaning over the lecture bench the while to seek out the intended recipient of his generous encomia. At last he could go on no longer and asked "Isn't Dirac here?" to which Paul Ehrenfest replied "Nur sein Loch." ("Only his hole.") About fifteen minutes later Dirac's puzzled countenance appeared around the door to the side of the lecture bench to the accompaniment of a roar of friendly laughter.

At my first meeting with Niels Bohr he asked if I had a place to live and referred me to a wonderful old lady Professorinde Maar, who in her widowed years supplemented her income by letting a room to one of his young physicists. She regarded herself as their *Pflegermutter* and them as her *Pflegerkinder* ("foster-mother" and "foster-children"). She had no paying guest at the time so she gladly took me in even though I was working with Martin Knudsen at the Polytechnic Institute on Sølvgaede and not at the Institute of Theoretical Physics on Blegdamsvej. From her apartment it was just a short cycle ride to Sølvgaede by way of Langelinie, where invariably every morning I would pass King Christian X, always alone, riding in the opposite direction on his horse. I have sometimes wondered if he missed the early morning cyclist on Langelinie when I left Copenhagen. Another of her *Pflegerkinder* was Werner Heisenberg who was returning to Germany from the United States via Copenhagen in August 1933 and was to play a Beethoven piano concerto in Berlin. He had been practising it in the United States and played one movement at a birthday party that Fru Maar gave for me. He also told us some risky, but not *risqué*, jokes about Hindenburg and Hitler. A few years later Heisenberg also gave me a "reference" to my future wife's relatives, Walter and Martha Colby, whom he had been visiting at the University of Michigan in 1933.

On my arrival in Copenhagen I had signed in at the British Legation. As I was rather a rare phenomenon, namely a British physicist on a long-term visit, I soon received an invitation to dine at the Legation from the British Minister and his wife, Sir Thomas and Lady Hohler. Here started a friendship that was renewed during the war, in England, after my wife Miriam and I returned from the United States in 1938. Sir Thomas had been Minister during World War I in Mexico and was instrumental in obtaining the notorious Zimmermann letter that played a large part in drawing the United States into the war. His account of that incident provided my first direct insight into that netherworld of intrigue and counter-intrigue.

The English church is located on Langelinie and I returned there in 1979, for a special service commemorating the victory of the Battle of Britain, in the company of Colonel Else Martensen-Larsen, ex-Commandant of the Royal Danish Womens' Air Force, who with her husband Oluf had welcomed me to Copenhagen nearly fifty years ago. In 1932 the minister of the church was Rev Bernard Everett, a minor canon of Windsor Chapel, and his wife had been most hospitable to me. As will be seen, we were to meet again later.

My research with Martin Knudsen at the Polytechnic Institute had been mainly concerned with the exchange of energy between gas molecules and solid surfaces (a topic which happened also to be of passing interest to Edward Teller, who was visiting Niels Bohr's Institute towards the end of my stay in Copenhagen). I returned to Imperial College in the Autumn of 1933 to take up an Assistant Lectureship. This enabled me to continue my research, and I was able to employ the newly discovered technique of electron diffraction, which G P Thompson had brought down with him from Aberdeen, to investigate the dependence of such energy exchanges upon the crystalline state of the solid surface. My work with Martin Knudsen was deemed sufficient to qualify me for the award in 1934 of a London doctorate of philosphy. One day in this period remains indelibly engraved upon my memory. It was 26 July 1934, the day after Dr Engelbert Dollfuss, Chancellor of Austria, was assassinated.

In Copenhagen I became friendly with another research student at the Polytechnic Institute, Peter Mathes, and, later, with his family who lived on a mountainous estate in Lower Austria that stretched up the Seethal from the head of the Lunzer See where their home, Schloss Seehof, two wings of which comprised a monastery warehouse that dates from 1601, was located. One of the mountain peaks that looks down on the Schloss, the Hetzkogel (1680 m), is the coldest spot in Western Europe, with temperatures dropping to −50°C in some hollows on the mountain in winter. Even as late as May the clouds touch the surrounding mountains and paint them and the fir trees with a light layer of snow. Peter's great-grandfather, Leopold Kupelwieser, was the friend and painter of Franz

Schubert, and painted the water colour "Schubert and his friends playing party-games at Atzenbrugg", now hanging in the Schubert Museum in Vienna.

In 1933 I visited the Schloss from Copenhagen during the summer vacation, and walked up the Seethal to the summit of the Dürrenstein. Next year I arranged to revisit Seehof accompanied by two St Paul's school friends, Hugh Cockburn and Geoffrey Dobbs, and we spent a few days prior to that walking in Bavaria and the Tyrol in the areas of Füssen and the Plansee. 25 July, the day of Dr Dollfuss's death, found us on the German side of the border and on 26 July, the day we planned to proceed to Lunz, we learned that the frontier had been closed by the Austrian Heimwehr.

Rather than interrupt our vacation schedule we decided to press on anyhow by way of a mountain ridge that would avoid the official points of entry. I shall never forget the successful cresting of the ridge and our joyous but reckless scramble down the other side into Austria, until an unexpected tumble where I had misjudged a steep drop brought us to our senses. Eventually, very tired and hungry, we came down to a cow-herder's hut where the kindly occupant gave us milk to drink. Nor shall I forget the unexpected pain as we gratefully gulped the milk through our parched throats.

We successfully reached Seehof, but the Nazi take-over of Austria had begun. Nevertheless, in those days there were still very many courageous Austrians who could tell anecdotes like the one about the two doctors who met one day: The one greeted his colleague with "Heil Hitler" (hail Hitler) and the other replied "Heile Du Ihn" (heal him yourself).

By 1936, however, I began to get footloose again and I applied successfully for a two-year Commonwealth Fund Fellowship. This I planned to hold at the University of California in Berkeley working in the Radiation Laboratory of Ernest O Lawrence whose cyclotron was achieving accelerations of protons, deuterons and helium ions to energies of several million electron volts. When such high-energy ions were used to bombard non-radioactive targets, nuclear transmutations were effected that resulted in the production of many new and interesting radioactive species. The possibilities opened up by such transmutations were capturing the scientific imagination at that time, one possibility in particular being that, since accomplished, of reproducing long-since defunct, or decayed, transuranic elements.

So, on 11 August 1936, another Commonwealth Fellow, J Campbell Hornel, and I arrived in New York aboard the Cunard liner *Scythia*. It was for me the first and slowest of about one hundred one-way Atlantic crossings. Some ten days later, after visiting Professor and Mrs E A Uehling at the University of Michigan, I arrived in Berkeley on the streamliner *City of San Francisco* carrying all necessary credentials, including an introduction to the girl who subsequently became my wife.

In Berkeley I found that there were three main aims in life. In order of priority these were to keep the cyclotron going 24 hours a day, to carry on research when another "crew" was running the cyclotron, and to keep ourselves sane and healthy by skiing in Yosemite or Lake Tahoe in winter, or enjoying the splendour of the cacti in Death Valley, or parties on the beach in spring or summer. Somewhere I still have a movie of that wizard of physics R W Wood doing experiments in the sand when the whole laboratory shut down for the day and we all took him to a beach near Mt Tamalpais. If, on the other hand, the cyclotron shut down for longer than five minutes when you were on the night shift, you could expect a telephone call from Ernest Lawrence (who had a radio receiver at home that tuned into the radio frequency of the cyclotron) to ask if we were having problems. Life was a combination of hard work and great fun, in both of which Ernest joined with zest and enthusiasm.

There were also many parties at the homes of my colleagues. Among them were several "drawing-room communists", for at that time feelings ran high over the Spanish Civil War. I use the term drawing-room communist because so often the most ardent discussions took place in comfortable living rooms with plenty of liquor on hand. The atmosphere was not peculiar to Berkeley at that time, but was typical of the ambience of those not too far left of centre who viewed the onslaught of fascism with abhorrence and disgust. Those at the far left went in the 1930s and fought in Spain. Those not so far to the left, who discussed and theorized in comfort, probably prepared the ground for those in the 1940s who broke their allegiance and took the law into their own hands to help an ally. But not all our evenings were spent in political discussion. I remember especially the way in which the Commonwealth Fellows at the University of California, five or six of us in all, were made welcome by Professor Craig, a Scotsman who taught in the English department, and Mrs Craig. Whenever we were invited to their house we knew we should find steak-and-kidney pie prepared for us as a special treat—whether we liked it or not. I happened not to, but this did not prevent me from enjoying their hospitality.

In the Radiation Laboratory one of the most prolific pastimes was to look for radioactive isotopes of the different stable elements produced by ion bombardment in the cyclotron. Many of us would have an interest in particular bombarding particles incident upon particular stable targets. Thus some were interested in producing transuranic elements. My work was the investigation of nuclear reactions produced by the bombardment of copper and zinc with helium ions, and I was able to identify several radioactive isotopes of gallium and germanium. One of them, gallium-67, had become a widely used radiopharmaceutical within the last few years. For the period January to June 1937 I was appointed "Voluntary Teaching Assistant in Physics without salary" and gave a course in elementary physics to first-year students. Their academic ability, however, did not always seem to be up to that of their contemporaries at the Imperial College.

In the summer vacation between the two academic years of the Fellowship we were expected to spend about two months seeing America. So in 1937 Campbell Hornel and I set off in a small Chevrolet coupé to cover as much of the country as we could. We travelled by way of the Grand Canyon to New Orleans, north to New England and Niagara, west to Seattle and Victoria—a journey of about 20,000 miles in all. Other people's travelogues are as dull as other people's family photographs unless drama intervenes, and the nearest we came to that was when a bear I was photographing in Yellowstone Park got hold of my leg. Perhaps because I weighed only 140 lb in those far-off days, he quickly lost interest and let go of it. It is enough to say then that we did not realize until later our good fortune in being able to make such a kaleidoscopic survey of what is a continent rather than a country so soon before world events put extended holidays like this out of the question.

Something far more fortunate, far more important, happened to me personally in that same year of 1938. I have mentioned above an introduction given to me by the Uehlings to their friend Miriam Tueller who was also at the University of California, Berkeley, studying economics. We became engaged about one year later and were married on 4 August 1938. She had chosen my birthday for the occasion, thinking that it might make it easier for me to remember the anniversary each year; but her strategem has been somewhat less than highly successful.

Perhaps here I can conveniently clear the "family photographs" out of the way by saying that we have been blessed with three children, each of whom is leading a happy and worthwhile life. Kris, our elder daughter, is like her husband Rick, a PhD of McGill. They hold similar posts as associate professors of biology at the University of Alaska and each of them has recently received a substantial grant for research from the National Institutes of Health. They have two children, Jessie and Max. Our son Peter, after a couple of years as a boarder at an English school (Abingdon), also graduated (in Mathematics) from McGill. He works in computer systems engineering in Montreal where he lives with his wife Judy and their little daughter Lucy. Janet, our younger daughter, after National Cathedral School, graduated in Music from Goucher College in Baltimore, and then took a master's degree in Education at Towson University. Besides being a very compenent pianist, she plays a number of games, and had an Olympics trial for hockey. She is now a physical education teacher.

2
England

We returned to England on the *Queen Mary* in early September 1938, and found a small flat in St Catherine's Court at Turnham Green, in West London. By the end of September the British fleet had been mobilized, air-raid trenches were being dug outside our kitchen window, and we had been issued gas masks against the eventuality of war following Neville Chamberlain's negotations in Berchtesgaden, Godesberg and Munich.

I returned to the Imperial College as lecturer in charge of the third-year physics laboratory, a position which I held, with some inter-ruptions, until 1946. On my return G P Thomson and I naturally discussed the possibility of building a cyclotron at the Imperial College, but we found that such a project was beyond our means. Instead, in the early summer of 1939, we settled for a less ambitious two-million-volt Van de Graaff electrostatic accelerator to study nuclear reactions. Accordingly, G P obtained a Royal Society grant for the purpose of my visiting Professor Raymond Herb's laboratory in Madison, Wisconsin, to obtain information from him about the design of such accelerators. This visit took place in August 1939, but in the meantime, having obtained Ernest's permission, I busied myself with writing a monograph about the cyclotron[1]* and with preparing courses of lectures in acoustics and thermodynamics.

*Superscript numbers refer to Reference at the end of the book (pp. 136).

In July 1939 we spent a brief holiday in Copenhagen and then I left for Madison, Wisconsin, leaving Miriam to hike around the island of Bornholm with my cousin, Dr Trevor Mann. He spent the later years of the then imminent war as surgeon-lieutenant in destroyers working with the Atlantic and Arctic convoys, and he has just retired from the post of senior paediatrician at the Royal Alexandria Hospital for Children in Brighton. I sailed on the Polish-Amerika liner *Batory* from Copenhagen and arrived in New York on 2 August, 1939. But as we were sailing west the war clouds were beginning to gather in the east and there was much speculation whether the *Batory* would make it back to Gdynia before the outbreak of hostilities. The captain, however, was quoted as saying that he was not frightened of Hitler's submarines and would take his ship back; he feared only two things, the one was God and the other his wife. One month later when I was in New York trying to get a ship home I learned that the *Batory* was still there and had been moved to a berth up the Hudson River.

Meanwhile I had cabled, from Madison, to our Danish friends asking them to urge Miriam and Trevor to return to England as quickly as possible. Fortunately they took my advice and they arrived home before the outbreak of war; but 3 September found me still in Boston visiting the laboratory of Robert Van de Graaff. When I reached New York I found the trans-Atlantic departures in a state of chaos. I obtained a reservation on the Holland-Amerika liner *Nieuw Amsterdam* to Plymouth and actually boarded her and settled into a very pleasant cabin. A few minutes before we were due to sail, however, the sailing was postponed for an hour and the stop in Plymouth cancelled. Rather than go on to Rotterdam I retrieved my ticket, disembarked, and returned to the home of relatives of Miriam's in New Jersey. There I stayed while I tried to book a passage home; after a few days I secured a reservation on the United States Lines *SS Manhattan*. With about one hour left to catch the ship I was driven at high speed to the dock and boarded the vessel with just five minutes to spare before the scheduled time for sailing. As the ship was lightly loaded and was expecting to be returning from Europe overfilled with American tourists, they had taken ballast on board in New York. This ballast was alleged to be copper, a material that could be assumed to be useful for the war effort, thereby indicating the direction of American sympathy even in the first few days of the war.

A large proportion of the crew was, however, of German origin (US citizens but with families still in Germany) and they walked off the ship rather than take the risk of running contraband. This could have been typical ship's rumour, but our departure was certainly delayed for six hours. Nevertheless, I still had a German table steward and a Swedish cabin steward, each of whom was equally confident that Britain could in no way survive the German onslaught. These depressing forecasts were reinforced by the news that the Cunarder *Athenia* had been torpedoed and sunk. My old friend John Lawrence (Ernest's brother) who was returning on the *Athenia* from a British Association meeting was missing for several days.* (He was, I believe, the first, with Joseph Hamilton, to use the radioactive isotope of phosphorus—phosphorus 32—for the clinical treatment of leukaemia in the late 1930s.) The atmosphere was therefore gloomy on board the *Manhattan* and many passengers elected to sleep on deck close to the life rafts as we proceeded with large, fully flood-lit Stars and Stripes painted on the port and starboard sides of the hull. When we landed in Southampton steel-helmeted Tommies lined the path from the gangway to the passport and customs shed. The change in the two months since we had left for Denmark was hard to believe.

I reported back to the Imperial College and was surprised to find that classes were to proceed "as usual". Some other colleges of the University of London were to be evacuated to the country, but we were to continue teaching students provided that they engaged in some form of civil-defence work, as special constables or air-raid wardens or the like in their "spare time". One of the basement corridors was sandbagged, with a blackboard at each end, and to these we adjourned from either of the physics lecture rooms upstairs whenever an air-raid alert was sounded. Actually these circumstances combined to give our students a more serious concern in their work. I remember hearing of one of our students who, on the night of a concentrated raid on the Fulham power station, was rudely awakened by a bomb falling through the house where he was lodging. He got out of bed, fell through a hole in the floor and found himself sitting on the bomb in the basement.

---

*Letter of 9 September 1939, from Professor Ernest Lawrence to W B Mann, p 137 in Appendix A.

Petrified, he nevertheless managed to remove himself from the bomb. The unexploded bomb section cleared the neighbourhood and fifteen minutes later his lodgings were completely obliterated.

Soon after my return G P Thomson decided that we should do everything possible to keep our group of seven highly skilled mechanics in the physics workshop together as a team that might in future do valuable work for a department such as the Ministry of Aircraft Production. For some time the Medical Research Council (MRC) had been considering the installation of a two-million-volt Van de Graaff high-voltage electrostatic generator (or accelerator) to produce high-energy electrons and positive ions for investigating the biological effects of neutrons, electrons and x rays. It was therefore decided in the autumn of 1939 to build two such generators at the Imperial College, and it was arranged for L G Grimmett, of the MRC Unit at Hammersmith Hospital, to join me to work on them. This would give us a means of keeping our whole group occupied making the necessary parts. All normal research work had stopped in the physics department, and I soon found the head of the workshop, Mr A E Davis, following me like a hungry horse and demanding drawings of the parts for the generators which we had not yet even started to design. It happened, however, that each generator had a column of about seventy insulated rings, each about three feet in diameter, each supported by three carefully machined bakelite insulators. This made a total requirement of more than 400 insulators for the two generators. I hastily made a drawing of an insulator, not unlike the cylindrical porcelain electrical insulators with corrugated sides that are commonly seen, and asked Mr Davis to make 420 of these with some spares. By the time the suitable cutting tools had been made for the grooved sides and some 450 insulators had been produced, we had managed to make drawings of some other part and so we kept ahead of the workshop until late 1940 or early 1941, when more important work on behalf of the war effort gradually displaced the construction of the Van de Graaff accelerators from the Imperial College workshop. Work on the Imperial College accelerator resumed in 1945[2], but in the meantime. Professor J W Boag and Dr P Howard Flanders continued construction of the MRC accelerator at Hammersmith Hopsital.

As far as my own career was concerned, I had had my small

monographs on the cyclotron published on 25 January 1940[1]; Ernest Lawrence welcomed it with typical enthusiasm.* Then in July 1940 I was offered a job at the Admiralty Research Establishment at Swanage, but the Imperial College was not willing to release me from the work in which I was then engaged.† At about that time I was also elected to the Council of the Physical Society and appointed General Editor of its *Report on Progress in Physics* with the request that I try to keep it going "for the duration". This I managed to do with the help of many American and British friends who generously contributed articles. Every one of these kind contributors from both sides of the Atlantic gave his time as a personal favour and one, Max Born, contributed two articles. Between us all we produced three volumes covering respectively the years 1941, 1942–3 and 1944–5. Miriam worked at home on the author indices of the first two volumes and Dr Frances Lowater prepared the index for the third volume. At the end of the war I handed my responsibilities over to a whole Board of Editors.

But this is looking ahead. The so-called "phoney" war had suddenly become real. The evacuation of Dunkirk was completed on 4 June. That evening at home we thrilled to the words of Winston Churchill: "We shall fight on the beaches ... in the fields or in the hills; we shall never surrender."

After all these years it is difficult to recapture, still more difficult to communicate to a younger generation, what life was like in London, from 10 July 1940, which was the first day of what we later knew as the Battle of Britain, until 2 November of the same year, which was the last night of the fifty-seven continuous nights of bombing. During the Battle of Britain I often watched the weaving trails of the fighter planes as I stood in the manually operated door of a District Line train between Turnham Green and Hammersmith Stations *en route* to work in the morning. For the first week of the "blitz" we adjourned during the alarms to the air-raid shelter in a nearby block of flats. One night a bomb fell twenty or thirty feet away and the ground heaved but the building withstood the shock. One of our fellow shelterers was a refugee from

---

*Letter of 5 April 1940, from Professor Ernest Lawrence to W B Mann, p 138 in Appendix A.

†Letter of 11 July 1940, from Mr F Brundrett to W B Mann, p139 in Appendix A.

Austria and it was symptomatic of the tolerance of Londoners that he could digress at length on the half-hearted British war effort and how the German bombers were better than the English bombers (pronounced with two b's as in "bombastic"). After a few nights in this shelter the anti-aircraft guns opened fire for the first time and it was like music to our ears.

One week of shelter night life was, however, all we could take and we decided to stay in the comfort of our own flat in St Catherine's Court. There we fell into the routine of eating by 7.30 pm and then settling in for an eleven-hour period during which the bombers seemed to cruise around dropping a desultory bomb just to keep us on our toes. I recollect that one night our routine was completely wrecked by the bombers arriving some two hours late; then occasionally the action was a little livelier as we were located about a quarter of a mile down the road from the Napier aeroplane engine plant. In the mornings on the way to work, the other passengers in the Turnham Green to South Kensington trip looked weary and worn out, but there was a friendship and comradeship that I have never known in London, before or since. It was an experience that we were proud to have shared and which we would never wish to have missed. But we were tired, very tired. We wondered how long we could endure the fatigue and then suddenly some respite came. Hit-and-run daylight and night-time raids continued, however, and I remember riding to Hammersmith one morning after the District Line had been hit the previous night, clinging to the 2-inch or 3-inch high railing along the side of a flat-top lorry designed to take railway containers and large crates. Near Hammersmith we ran into what appeared to be some low-flying machine-gun attack and the driver took several turns at a more than comfortable speed.

During this time Miriam was helping a couple of days a week at the Rainbow Club in Piccadilly, which had been established for Americans who had gone north to volunteer to serve in the Canadian armed forces. One unit of the RCAF, the Eagle Squadron, consisted entirely of such volunteers. She remembers having to stop these young Americans from spreading hot English mustard so thickly on their hot dogs that they yelped with pain when they bit into them.

About half-way through the main blitz our friends Gordon and Gunborg Sutherland invited us to spend a restful week-end in

Cambridge. I could not get away until the Saturday so I arranged to take Miriam to King's Cross on the Friday evening to link up with Gordon and travel to Cambridge with him. It happened to be the evening when the tube stations were opened as air-raid shelters for the first time and there was such chaos that we missed the train. Gordon had waited for us, however, and I managed to put them on a later train from Liverpool Street. I shall always remember that as I left the station to return home I saw what looked like a beautiful sunset—in the East. The Luftwaffe had been dropping fire bombs as markers that afternoon, and this glow was the harbinger of a massive raid on the docks. I was not sorry to reach Cambridge the next day, where I was greeted in the evening by a small raid—the first on the city—which was alleged by Germany to be in retaliation for a raid on Heidelberg. In spite of this we felt so relaxed by our short break in Cambridge that on our return we had to get used all over again to the London raids. This was a not uncommon phenomenon. There were some who refused the offer of a night out of London so as not to break their pattern.

When, however, my friends from my Copenhagen days, Canon and Mrs Everett, found us a small one-room cottage on Chinnor Hill, just on the western edge of the Chilterns, we gave up our London flat. During the week I bedded down on a mattress in the Imperial College and was glad to join Miriam at Chinnor for two or three nights of less broken sleep at the weekends. This gave us the chance of helping our neighbours immediately above us at St Catherine's Court. They were a Lithuanian family, the husband having been originally attached to the Legation in London. When the Red Army invaded Lithuania in June 1940, they elected to leave the Legation and remain in England with their two-year-old daugher. They were desperately poor and lived mainly on potatoes. When we went to Chinnor, Miriam would go foraging, and every weekend that I went there I would bring back half-a-dozen eggs, which I would take round to the flat for their baby on the following Wednesday evening. They always invited me to stay for supper, which invariably took the form of potato hamburger, often preceded by potato soup and followed by potato pancake. One Wednesday evening Mrs J said with considerable feeling, "Meester Mann, I am *seek* of potatoes!" I must say that I shared her sentiments, even though I shared the meal with them only once a week.

One Wednesday evening when I was delivering the eggs a major raid started, so I hurriedly bade farewell and took my departure. I was walking up Exhibition Road and I had almost reached the College when there was a crash behind me. Two or three cyclists had just passed and I went back thinking that one of them might have fallen. I walked back about 40 or 50 feet and in the black-out almost stumbled over a steel-helmeted Bobby outside the Science Museum. Rather confusedly I asked "Did someone fall off?" "No", he replied, "this bloody nearly got me", and showed me the very sizeable head of an anti-aircraft shell. I lost no time covering the remaining 100 yards to the College; next day I timed my transit back to the small conical cavity made by the shell in the pavement and found that I had passed over the spot about ten seconds before hearing the crash.

Next Wednesday a large-scale raid again interrupted our after-supper conversation, so I rose to leave and asked if our friends could lend me a thick book. Mrs J kindly produced an approximately three-inch-thick copy of their Lithuanian Bible and insisted that I take it. I remember walking slowly, and I hope with dignity, up Exhibition Road with the Bible balanced on my felt hat, feeling doubly secure both from the thickness and the nature of the book. Next week I returned it, unharmed and undamaged, to our friends.

Such was life in London. On one occasion Miriam and I went to hear Ida Händel play the Beethoven Violin Concerto in D at the Queen's Hall. She went on playing during a brief air-raid alert and then at the conclusion of the concert we left the hall to find another alert in progress. We walked down Regent Street to Piccadilly Circus Station in the black-out, stumbling over the sand bags placed over the glass blocks in the pavement that lighted the cellars. In the blackout we found ourselves walking around consciously looking out of the corners of our eyes in order to utilise the greater sensitivity of peripheral vision. About a week later the Queen's Hall was burned out by incendiaries, and we gave up the effort of trying to spend an evening out in London.

By "sleeping rough" in the Imperial College I found I was brought into very close—and pleasant—relationship with G P Thomson because he also frequently camped out at the College. I had a very pleasant small office adjoining the third-year physics laboratory with a fire-place and a small supply of coal; and usually before retiring he would drop into my office for an hour or two and we would sit in front of the fire discussing physics, the war and atomic energy. Professor Rudolph Peierls had suggested a possible method of enriching uranium, and I was given the task of trying to develop a small experimental device to test it, with the help of Mr Davis and his colleagues in the physics workshop. At about this time I also took over G P's lectures in nuclear physics in addition to my own in acoustics and thermodynamics, as he was becoming more and more involved with the work of scientific advisory committees. In March 1941 G P became chairman of the so-called M.A.U.D. Technical Committee. As I was already involved in work with Professor Peierls I was invited to serve on it. The letter of invitation* came from my old friend and co-author, Basil Dickins, who was now in the Directorate of Scientific Research of the Ministry of Aircraft Production.

At the end of 1940 one happier event intervened to take our minds away from the gloomy business of war. Ernest Lawrence was awarded the Duddell Medal of the Physical Society of London. This was to have been presented to him by Lord Lothian at a dinner of the American Physical Society on 27 December 1940, in Philadelphia but because of Lord Lothian's sad and sudden death the presentation was made by the British Chargé d'Affaires, Mr Neville Butler. On the same day, in London, the Physical Society held a luncheon to celebrate the occasion of the award and I was invited to propose Ernest's health.† My remarks on that occasion formed the basis for an article in the January 1941 *Proceedings of the Physical Society*.[3] I should like to quote a short passage from it:

> Incredulity is one of the most common reactions to the performance of the Berkeley cyclotrons. But to know Ernest Lawrence is to know too why it is that the Berkeley cyclotrons give such incredible results. In the face of such irrepressible enthusiasm and such *joie de vivre* difficulties hardly stand a chance, and faced too by his deep innate *sense* of physics they merely stand to fall. And in trying to appreciate that irresistible drive in the laboratory

---

*Letter of 23 March 1941, from Dr B G Dickins to W B Mann, p 140 in Appendix A.
†Letter of 2 March 1942, from Professor Ernest Lawrence to W B Mann, p 141 in Appendix A.

one cannot but recall the boisterous enthusiasm of Lawrence away from work. He might return from a ski-trip with an injured arm or be hobbling around the laboratory with a stick for some days after; but so soon as the opportunity returned he would launch himself as joyously as before over the brink of some snow-clad slope. One also recalls wildly happy days (equally unreal and like some far-off pleasant dream!) on some Pacific beach or in his motor-cruiser on San Francisco Bay. 'Ernest carries a chart in his boat', said one of his friends, 'so that he'll know what mud-bank he is stranded on.'

At about this time I also remember working one evening at the Imperial College in the Physics Department drawing office, with its tall glass windows, making a drawing of the next part of the Van de Graaff accelerator to be made in the workshop. There had been no air-raid alert but suddenly I became aware of the familiar whistle of a falling bomb. I ducked under the drawing table and spent I suppose just a few seconds, it seemed longer, alternately cursing and praying. The bomb dropped about a quarter of a mile away, but I never saw exactly where.

In the spring of 1941, under the strain of the hit-and-run raids, I began to feel dissatisfied with my work on the uranium project, and I went to discuss it with the Rector of Imperial College, Sir Henry Tizard. Sir Henry had been chairman of the Technical Sub-Committee of the Air Defence Research Committee since the mid-1930's and had, I understood, played a great part in pushing the development of the Spitfire and of Robert Watson-Watt's radio direction finding, each of which had stood us in good stead in the Battle of Britain. I told him that I could not believe that an atom bomb would be developed in time to win the war against Germany and I felt I ought to get into other work more directly concerned with our main objective. Sir Henry agreed and so I entered into negotiations with the Ministry of Supply in May 1941 with a view to working at the Ministry in London while continuing to give my lectures at the Imperial College. I started work at the Ministry on 12 May, although the correspondence showed that the negotiations continued until 29 June in order to clarify whether or not my work at the College constituted "an outside interest"! In the end I remained a member of the College staff, seconded to the Ministry as a temporary civil servant. From then on I spent about 95 per cent of my working hours at the Ministry of Supply. In the meantime Russia was invaded on 21 June 1941, and despite the inherent horror of it all, we felt the relief from a dissipation of the enemy pressure in other directions.

The headquarters of the Ministry of Supply's Directorate of Scientific Research (DSR) was at Shell Mex House on the Strand. After my part-time assignment there we decided to abandon Chinnor and find ourselves once more a home in London. Miriam went flat hunting, concentrating on flats in fairly new steel and concrete buildings. In September 1941 we settled into a fifth-floor flat in Belvedere Court on Upper Richmond Road, Putney, whence the Strand was easily accessible by means of a short walk to Putney Station, a train from there to Waterloo, and another short walk across Waterloo Bridge.

For the next two years life was pretty hectic. First I would start work in the morning at Shell Mex House, and then one or two days a week during term time I would take a taxi to the Imperial College to give a one-hour lecture. Then by cab back to the Ministry to spend the afternoon on the applications of science to warfare; I went home in the evenings for dinner and then, often past midnight, I ended the day with work on examination papers, *Reports on Progress in Physics,* or just in fire watching on the roof.

I was attached initially to SR1, the general-physics branch of DSR. The work in this branch was concerned with subjects such as artillery sound ranging, simulated anti-aircraft gun flashes and infra-red techniques. I did not stay long in this department. For one thing, the work was not very exciting or challenging and, for another, Alexander King, my old friend and colleague from the Imperial College, needed a physicist in the branch of which he was Assistant Director, SR7, which covered all imperial and foreign liaison in scientific developments in the Ministry of Supply; this was, as its name implies, responsible for the provision of military resources and equipment. Our scientific interests, therefore, lay in such fields as radar, explosives and ammunition, artillery, infra-red devices, chemical warfare defence, anti-landmine devices, and so on. Our clients were all allied governments, imperial and foreign, including the governments in exile. Until Pearl Harbor, the rule governing the release of information to United States representatives was simple, namely if they asked for non-operational information we could release it, but if it were for some matter that involved current of future operations we had to seek special permission from the service, or services, involved.

During this period my overseas liaison contacts included a couple of very friendly U.S. lieutenant-colonels who were freezing with the cold that English winter. They wore civilian clothes until 8 December 1941, when they blossomed into full military regalia. Occasionally our meat ration would stretch to four lamb chops in a week and we would ask them to dinner, and they would respond with an invitation to their flat in Park Lane. Their fare was distinctly more sustaining, however, than that which we had been able to offer them. On one such evening they told us that they had just returned from visiting a British colonel in Liverpool and that he had shown them to the bathroom and told them to go ahead with a bath as there was plenty of hot water. It was winter, damp and cold, and feeling that they would have frozen if they had shed their long johns they decided to forego the luxury.

After 12 May 1941, when I went to work at the Ministry of Supply, I had not, as far as I remember, taken any part in the work of the M.A.U.D. Technical Committee, but I had apparently remained a member of it. In October 1941 it was agreed, following the suggestion of President Roosevelt to Prime Minister Churchill, to combine the American and British nuclear-energy programmes. In December the M.A.U.D. Committees were disbanded* and responsibility for the British side of the programme was vested in what was discreetly called the Directorate of Tube Alloys. Thus ended my association with nuclear physics until the end of the war, although I had an unexpected reminder some two or three years later when I heard a colonel in a Washington bar discussing the progress that had been made. The information probably meant more to me than to the rest of the company, but I regretfully reported the indiscretion to James Chadwick who was then also in Washington, and I learned another two or three years later from him that the colonel had been admonished on the merits of talking less about such matters.

I cannot remember exactly when I had moved over to Alexander King's Imperial and Foreign Liaison branch, but it must have been some

*Letter of 22 December 1941, from the Minister of Aircraft Production to W B Mann, p 142 in Appendix A.

time in the late summer or autumn of 1941, as the German armies were trying to break through the Russian resistance around Moscow. At that time two technical members of the Russian Trade Delegation were designated to liaise with us in connection with military supplies that were being sent to Russia. The name of one of them escapes me, but the one who seemed the more fluent was, I believe, a Mr Ershov. Anyhow, I recollect that about the time that the position of Moscow was at its most critical, the three of us had dinner together in a small restaurant in South Kensington. A number of Mark II radars had been sent to Russia for use in the air defence of Moscow, and three of four British Army majors had gone with them to give technical assistance. After the radar equipment had been located at suitable sites around Moscow and Russian personnel had been indoctrinated in their use, the British officers asked to visit the sites to give the operators any further assistance that they might require, but their offer was refused. Shortly thereafter I understood that these officers were withdrawn as it was pointless to leave them in Moscow with nothing to do.

Discussing anything with Mr Ershov was like playing a game of chess, and the discussion at dinner that night centred on this Mark II radar equipment and Mr Ershov asked me a number of questions about it. Suddenly he asked me "And how does that compare with the Mark III?" I replied that there *was* no Mark III. "But", he said, "the workers in the factory have told us there is." I knew that a Mark IIIX (X for experimental) was being tested at Christchurch, but was also pretty sure that none was yet in production, so I simply shrugged my shoulders and said that I was sorry but there were no Mark IIIs. Subsequently I heard that one of the unfortunate majors had been caught off guard with the same question.

A short time later (and it seemed so incongruous with Moscow still under siege and its citizens suffering such privations), Mr Ershov and his friend entertained me to lunch at "A l'Ecu de France" in Jermyn Street; they were greatly amused that their *bête noire,* General Sikorski, the Prime Minister of the Polish Government in exile, was sitting at a neighbouring table!

One of the most satisfying working relationships that I had during this period from late 1941 until mid-1943 was with Professor Leif Tronstad, a physical chemist from Trondheim and now at the Royal Norwegian

Army Headquarters in Kensington Gore. Professor Tronstad was described by William Stevenson in his book *A Man Called Intrepid* as the "key Baker Street Irregular in future atomic missions", but our joint interests lay in much more mundane matters. In March 1945 Leif Tronstad was murdered by quislings in northern Norway. On the twentieth anniversary of his death I was asked to write a short tribute to his memory for the journal *Fra Fysikkens Verden* of the Norweigian Physical Society. Perhaps I may quote from that article in describing our work together.

It is twenty years this month (March, 1965) since our very good friend Professor Leif Tronstad lost his life in the course of a commando expedition to his native land of Norway which he understandably loved so well. ...

We were priviliged to know him for two of the most critical years of the War during which we benefited from his well organized and expeditious supply of Norwegian technical talent whenever it was needed. On one occasion we had a need for three carbide-furnace experts. Three were available in Norway and after I had conveyed the request for their services to Dr. Tronstad they were in London within three or four days. At another time, when I was visiting him at the Royal Norwegian Army headquarters, he had just received, from the leader of the expedition, the report of the demolitions at the heavy water plant at Rjukan which had been accomplished only some two days previously after, as he told me, a journey by the expedition of some 1200 km on ski in full army uniform! Major Tronstad was very poud of this. On another occasion he called me to tell me that Dr. Vogt, the Rector of Trondheim University, had arrived in town after flying across the North Sea in a Mosquito fighter-bomber. Dr. Vogt came to our flat in London for tea, as in those days it was difficult to find enough protein to entertain for dinner, and he told us that only three days before he had been hiding in an attic in Oslo and had seen the R.A.F. Mosquitoes come in at eye level to bomb the Gestapo headquarters. Tragically the building was directly hit, so he said, by two bombs one of which penetrated the basement but failed to explode, while the other went through the building and exploded near a street-car killing twenty Norwegians. We managed to find a position for Dr. Vogt in the Ministry of Aircraft Production.

On another occasion I remember Leif Tronstad asking me if I could find useful war work for a bright young Norwegian (then a scientist) in America named Gunnar Randers. If so, he would bring him to England. I approached J D Cockcroft and obtained an assurance of employment at the Air Defence Research and Development Establishment, the British Ministry of Supply radar establishment. When the then Major Randers arrived his security clearance had not been completed, so he occupied my office at the Imperial College of Science and Technology for some three months, amusing himself with technical problems.*

It was a privilege to be invited by Leif Tronstad to attend the Norwegian National Day celebrations at the Albert Hall on May 17, 1943. Crown Prince Olav was present and the principal speaker was Sir Archibald Sinclair, Secretary of State for Air, who announced the destruction of the Möhne dam the night before, in which operation units of the Royal Norwegian Air Force had participated. ....

There was one very private aspect of Leif Tronstad's life into which I never inquired. He frequently went to Scotland to practise parachute jumping. I suspected that he did not always come down in Scotland but I never asked.

A letter to me from Leif Tronstad†, after I left London for Washington, tells something more of him and that fine group, Major Helmer Dahl, Captain C A Fürst, Captain Halvorsen, Miss Vold and others whom I did not know, who were members of his team. The last sentence of his letter sums up his deep loyalty and his great hope:

'We are still doing our best, which of course is not very much, but are longing for our real home more than ever.'

Leif Tronstad returned home, in March 1945.[4]

---

*In the placing of these scientists and in obtaining their necessary clearances I always had the very friendly help and expert guidance of the then Dr C P Snow, who was Director of the Technical Division of the Ministry of Labour from 1940 to 1944.

†Letter of 2 February 1944, from Professor Leif Tronstad to W B Mann, p 143 in Appendix A.

Miss Vold was Gerd Vold who was later the land-based secretary of the Kontiki expedition. I still treasure the envelope addressed to her from a Norwegian ship at sea with Norwegian Government-in-exile stamps that she gave to me before leaving for the U.S.A. in 1943. If any of those old friends and comrades should read these words, it would be wonderful to hear from them again.

Some time in the summer or autumn of 1942 my good friend Alex King left the Ministry of Supply to join the Office of the Scientific Advisers in the Ministry of Production that had been created in February 1942. I was asked to take charge of the branch in an acting capacity and for the next nine months I ran the branch, gave my lectures at the Imperial College and, in joint endeavour, Miriam and I between us produced a 350-page 1941 Volume VIII of the *Reports on Progress in Physics* and a 7 lb 1 oz offspring, Kristine Elizabeth. (To save two words in the cabled announcement to Miriam's mother, we gave the weight as 113 oz but, to her mother's horror, the first digit got lost in transmission.) In our spare time we had dug up a small portion of a hard-as-rock local soccer field to form an "allotment" where we grew very welcome fresh vegetables, including Indian corn. In the middle of summer, with the help of two hours of wartime daylight saving, it was an interesting experience to find ourselves tending our vegetables as late as eleven o'clock at night.

By this time, after such an orgy of creativity without any break of vacation, we were both exhausted and I was warned by the doctor that if I carried on at the same pace I risked a breakdown. About the time that Kris was nine months old we also had an unpleasant experience, that had nothing to do however with our general feeling of fatigue. A small air raid occurred one night, probably in June, and flares had been dropped slightly to the east of us. There was a strong east wind blowing and the flares brilliantly lit up the houses backing on to the Putney-to-Barnes railway that skirted the north end of our block of flats. The effect was quite dramatic; the backs of the houses looked like a flat two-dimensional stage setting. We were leaning out of our bedroom window, on the fifth floor facing east, entranced by the eerie beauty of the scene, when suddenly there was the familiar whistle of the falling bombs. No longer entranced, we ducked down to the floor to avoid the broken glass. The bombs fell some two to three hundred yards to the west, killed fourteen unfortunate neighbours and took out the water main. Kris was in a room the other side of the hall with a screen between the window and her crib, but we rushed into her room, removed her on her mattress, and left her in the hall for the rest of the night. No more bombs fell that night so we might just as well have left her to sleep on in her crib. Nor did any more fall in our locality for the rest of our time in England.

Even if heavy, the work in war-time scientific liaison had been interesting and rewarding. Early in 1943 thoughts began to turn to post-war reconstruction and I was asked to give my views on the employment of scientists, and also about initiating steps to assure an adequate supply of technical books to train them after the war. I gave my views directly on the former question* but wrote to our old friend Professor A V Hill to ask his advice about the books.†

One incident from my period with DSR sticks in my mind. The principal assistant to the head of the liaison branch was a Miss M Fry, a mathematics graduate from Ireland who was a trained secretary and one of the mainstays of the branch. One day she brought me a request from our US opposite numbers for technical details of our radar-directed searchlight. We decided that we ought to get official permission for the release of this information. So Miss Fry sent a hand-written minute to the Director of Royal Artillery over in the War Office. Some ten days later the minute sheet, much to Miss Fry's amusement, came back with a note from DRA referring the enquiry to General Staff, and another from General Staff to me, asking whether I, "as the expert in such matters", approved of the release. I responded by asking her to *type* a further minute still on the same sheet, for my signature, to say that I believed this to be in order. A week later back came the minute sheet again, with a note from General Staff to DRA and another from DRA to Miss Fry giving us the go-ahead.

There are two comments arising out of this story and they may conveniently close the chapter of my wartime experiences in this country. The first is that I could, and should, have made up my own mind in the first place. I had authority to do so, and if I had made a

*Letter of 3 March 1943, to Mr W E Dommett from W B Mann, p 144 in Appendix A.
†Letter of 21 April 1943, from Lord Hankey to Professor A V Hill, p 145 in Appendix A.

mistake the Minister of Supply would have backed me up publicly, whatever he might have said to me in private.

The second is that it illustrates the modern tendency to allow organizational structures and procedures to become the masters of scientific progress rather than its handmaidens—a tendency which in later years I found no less powerful in the United States Civil Service than in the British. In the 30 years since I joined the U.S. Civil Service—in many ways one of the best of its kind—my effective authority has diminished in inverse proportion to my promotion in rank.

If the nuclear chain promises unlimited power, the paper chain promises unlimited waste—of manpower, of time, of talent. One of the main weapons of the paper war is the photocopying machine, which by the sheer volume of its production can easily clog effectual communication. I sometimes play with the fantasy that we could promote a significant disaster in the Kremlin—perhaps even tip the scales in our direction—if we arranged to send the Russian establishment, free, as much photocopying equipment as they wanted.

3

Washington

It was in April or May of 1943 that I learned that a physicist was being sought to serve in the British Central Scientific Office (BCSO) in Washington. In this office scientists from the Dominions were gathered together to catalyse the exchange of information between the United States and the British Dominions. After the war it became the British Commonwealth Scientific Office and the acronym remained the same.

At this time both Miriam and I were feeling pretty well worn out and not only would this give her a break in her own country but it would give me one job to do instead of three. Volume IX of *Reports on Progress in Physics* for 1942–3 was due out in the second half of 1943 (I eventually wrote its Preface in September 1943) so, if someone would take over my lectures, I would then be available for other work. Of the three kind friends who helped me out, I can remember the name of only one, Dr R W B Stephens (Dr M Blackman and Dr W R Garton were probably the others); I did my best to make their job easier by leaving well-prepared notes for them.

So in early May I informed Dr H J Gough, Director-General of Scientific Research and Development in the Ministry of Supply, of my desire to resign. I do not have a copy of my letter to him, but there followed thereafter a very cordial correspondence. He replied at length on 14 May 1943, urging me to continue in the service of the Ministry.

The postscript to this letter and which might well have given me cause to change my mind, read: "I am convinced that the mere financial aspect has nothing whatever to do with your views; but you may like to know that, at the recent Promotion Board, the services you have rendered and are rendering are so well known and recognized, it was unanimously agreed to recommend you for promotion. This fact is a slight index, at any rate, of the esteem in which you are held by your scientific colleagues." I would not, in the normal course of events, have ever considered publishing these encomia but the fact that my services have been called into question overcomes my embarrassment. The rest of the story can be found in the offical correspondence.* In brief, my application was successful and I formally took up my new appointment on 30 June 1943. I was allowed to grade my examination papers at the Imperial College, then I spent part of my time in the Office of the Scientific Advisers of the Ministry of Production, and part of it in visiting those in the United Kingdom who would be most likely to be calling on my services in the United States. One on whom I called was Dr Alwyn Crow, of the Ministry of Supply, who showed me a reconnaissance photograph of Peenemünde in which a horizontally disposed V-2 rocket was clearly visible thereby affording me a first glimpse of a fore-runner of the space age. This was the first I knew of the existence of V-1s and V-2s, although the former were to enter very significantly into my life later in Washington.

After letting our flat Miriam, Kris and I boarded the RMS *Queen Mary* in Gourock on the afternoon of 4 September and sailed down the Clyde that night. Next morning we made our way down the St George's Channel with two cruisers slightly astern, the one to port and the other to starboard. On board there was military discipline. Under the Captain were American and British colonels in charge of the gun crews. There was an 8-pounder gun on the stern and about forty Bofors anti-aircraft guns on deck. We had a pep talk from the Captain who told us to carry our life jackets everywhere and that if anyone was caught smoking in any but the permitted places he would be very glad to put them in the

---

*Letter of 24 May 1943 from Dr H J Gough to W B Mann, p 146 in Appendix A.
Letter of 24 May 1943 from Dr H J Gough to Sir Edward Appleton, p 147 in Appendix A.
Letter of 27 May 1943 from Sir Edward Appleton to W B Mann, p 148 in Appendix A.
Letter of 1 July 1943 from Dr H J Gough to W B Mann, p 149 in Appendix A.

WASHINGTON 31

brig for the rest of the trip. We heard (another ship's rumour?) that two
or three junior military personnel in transit to the U.S. among the
passengers were meted out such treatment when found smoking in their
cabin.

The second night out the two cruisers disappeared and we were on a
pretty close zig-zag course—something like a nautical mile on each zig
or zag. But what a wonderful relaxation to be an sea again! At that time
the *Queen Mary* was essentially a troopship for American service men,
but a few of the upper-deck cabins had been refurbished to carry the
Prime Minister and his staff to the Quebec Conference on its previous
voyage west and we had a magnificent cabin that had been used by
Admiral Sir Dudley Pound. Our fellow travellers included the British
delegation to the Dumbarton Oaks Economics Conference and Lord
and Lady Keynes were our table companions. Lord Keynes assured us
that Kris, who became one year old three days after reaching the United
States, was now at the peak of her intellectual development, that she was
learning to walk and talk, and that her *rate* of intellectual development
(the *di/dt* of calculus) was greater at this time that it would ever be again.
Sir Edward Appleton, who had carried out the early experiments on the
ionosphere which led to radar and after whom the Appleton layer of the
inosphere was named, was also on board. I had the good luck to be
invited to join him on a thrilling visit to the bridge of the ship; we were
told that the only other civilian to be so honoured had been the Prime
Minister on the way to Quebec.

After a very pleasant voyage at speeds of 30 to 31 knots we arrived in
New York on 10 September, without ado or ceremony, and went
straight to Washington. There we stayed for a few days with friends in
Tauxemont on the Mount Vernon Highway in Virginia until we could
find a house to rent, which we soon did in the neighbourhood. On 7
October 1943 Professor Niels Bohr flew from Sweden to Scotland. A few
days later his son, Aage, followed on the Mosquito shuttle. Later in the
year both of them, father and son, reached the United States, and in the
early spring of 1944 they came to dinner with us in Tauxemont,
accompanied by a security officer who *insisted* that we address them by
their code names, Professor Baker and his son Jim Baker. In the course
of a very pleasant evening, "Jim" told us that he had recently been to
pick up his father's gold watch from the repair department of a

downtown Washington store. "How come", they asked, "that this watch was left for repair in the name of Professor Baker but is inscribed with the name of Niels Bohr?"

The BCSO was located on the 15th Street side of McPherson Square when I arrived but soon after moved to a mansion on the north-east corner of 17th Street, N.W. and Massachusetts Avenue. Associate-membership privileges were extended to me by the Cosmos Club and on one occasion when the family was away I spent two or three weeks in residence in its pleasant quarters that included the lovely Dolly Madison house on Lafayette Square.

As the only physicist at BCSO I had to deal with all matters classified as physics that came from Great Britian or America and to be available as needed for discussion and advice to the Dominion scientists in the office. Apart from that I was free to pursue or to develop contacts that I felt desirable and fruitful. T Taylor* sent a letter on 23 June 1943 to the Ministry of Production describing the kind of physicist needed at BCSO, and wrote "that the job will be one that he makes for himself. There is plenty to do if he is prepared to chase after it." I was soon in touch with the Office of Scientific Research and Development (OSRD) headed by Vannevar Bush, and its offspring, the National Defense Research Committee (NDRC), with the radio-proximity fuse laboratories of the American Army and Navy, and with the British service representatives in Washington. My job covered a wide spectrum of general physics, such as acoustics, electronics, infra-red and optics, but *no* nuclear physics.

Very soon after our arrival I became closely involved with the exchange of information between America and Britain on radio-proximity fuses, also code-named VT (for variable-time) fuses. The British effort in this direction had concentrated on fuses for rockets, while the American effort was directed towards the production of such fuses for bombs and shells. The last was by far the most difficult task because not only did the fuse have to withstand one enormous shock but it had to be quite small in terms of the size of radio components in the early 1940s.

The bomb fuse was being developed at the National Bureau of

---

*T W J (Tommy) Taylor was then Secretary of the Office but he resigned in 1944 and was succeeded by Alexander King as Director.

Standards on behalf of the United States Army by a group of which my principal contacts were Allen V Astin, Harry L Diamond, Alexander Ellett and William S Hinman. The laboratories where this work was conducted still function as the Harry Diamond Ordnance Laboratory, so named after the premature death of Harry Diamond in 1948.

The development of the shell fuse was, however, the responsibility of the United States Navy, and the work was carried on at the Applied Physics Laboratory (APL) of the Johns Hopkins University under what was known as a Section T contract with the Bureau of Ordnance of the Navy Department. The laboratory, which was referred to as APL or Section T, was under the direction of Merle A Tuve, who with Gregory Breit, in 1925,[5] described the method of radio-pulse sounding that was the fundamental principle underlying the development of radar. It was situated on Georgia Avenue in Silver Spring, Maryland, and I drove out there once or twice practically every week. My principal contact there was their roving ambassador, Professor Edward O Salent of New York University. My visits to APL became so frequent, in fact, that I was issued a pass that gave me unaccompanied access to the building. I eventually noticed that I was described as an American citizen on the pass. On pointing this out to the security office I was told, in effect, not to worry about such a minor detail when we were facing the exigency of fighting the same war. On one occasion I also accompanied a group down to Fort Bragg, North Carolina, to witness a most impressive test of howitzer VT fuses. Such fuses were subsequently used with tremendous effect in the "Battle of the Bulge" that began in December 1944 in the Ardennes.

Early in 1944 we received word that the flying bomb, the V-1, would soon be operational against London and Ed Salant urged that we make preparations to meet this threat. We asked Colonel William Brooks of the British Army Staff in Washington to get us any information he could about the V-1, but the War Office was not anxious to release it to us. Ed, however, was able to get some information from American sources on which he had a model of the flying bomb set up in New Mexico for sensitivity tests. The information he got was wrong in only one respect: the propulsive unit was thought to be under the flying bomb whereas it turned out to be on top. But the model was not that significantly different from what eventually turned out to be the real thing.

Therefore, having measured the required sensitivity, Merle Tuve, Larry Hafstad, Ed Salant and our friends in the Applied Physics Laboratory started producing adequate numbers of that type of fuse to meet the expected V-1 attack.

In the meantime Bill Brooks, Ed Salant and I constituted ourselves into an informal committee that met about once a week at the British Army Staff headquarters on 17th and K Streets NW, in Washington. From the context of Winston Churchill's description I believe that we were probably three of the "discerning experts" to whom he refers.*

Preparations for use of the VT fuse against the flying bomb seemed to be going well and Ed told me one day that the aircraft carrier HMS *Hermes* had been sent to pick up supplies of fuses with the higher sensitivity required for use against flying bombs. Then in the early hours of 13 June 1944, the first flying bombs hit Bethnal Green in London. But to the horror of our little committee we learned that the method of defence was for fighter aircraft to try to shoot down the bombs over the English Channel and then for the anti-aircraft guns to fire at them, using ordinary fuses, as they approached London. We could see no point in making doubly sure that they hit London, their primary target, by shooting them down in this way. In his subsequent account of this phase of the war General Pile (General Officer Commanding Anti-Aircraft Command) states that this Bethnal Green bomb may indeed have been shot down.† The Prime Minister notes that "(the defence) dispositions seemed sensible enough", but in no way did we at that time consider them to be rational. Ed, Bill and I felt strongly that the guns must be moved to the coast and must use radio-proximity fuses so that the flying bombs would be shot down into the sea. With the guns firing at low elevation at targets flying at altitudes of from 2000 to 3000 feet, these fuses could not be used over land for fear that if they failed to find a

---

*Winston S Churchill, *The Second World War,* Volume VI, pp 41 et seq (Cassell & Co Ltd, London 1954: "By the second week of July however General Pile and some discerning experts came to the conclusion that the guns could do very much better without undue prejudice to the success of the fighters if the batteries were moved on to the coast. Their Radar for fire control would have more scope, and it would be safer to use the proximity-fused shells which were now arriving from America."

†General Sir Frederick Pile, *ACK-ACK: Britain's Defence against Air Attack during the Second World War,* p 327 (George C Harrap & Co Ltd, London, 1949).

target or to destory themselves in the air they would detonate as they approached the ground, and could thus cause casualties among the civilian population.

The matter was so urgent that Bill decided to send one of his staff, Major Thompson, immediately to the United Kingdom to make our views known to General Pile. As the order to move the guns to the coast was not however given until 13 July, I presume that Major Thompson was able to communicate our views, but I must confess that in the hurly-burly of the next few weeks I did not even bother to ask.

In London, on the afternoon of 16 June, the Prime Minister met with Sir Archibald Sinclair (Secretary of State for Air), the Chiefs of Staff or their deputies, Air Chief Marshal Sir Arthur Tedder (Deputy Supreme Commander), Air Marshal Roderick Hill (Air Officer Commanding Air Defence of Great Britain) and General Pile. At this meeting it was decided that Hill, in consultation with Pile, should have the authority to re-deploy the defences "as necessary, to counter the attacks".*

Intensive discussions took place during the following four weeks; in this same period the launching sites of the bombs were themselves subjected to heavy bombing. Then on the evening of 13 July, after receiving reports that day from Air Commodore G H Ambler and Sir Robert Watson-Watt, and a conference in the early evening with General Pile and his staff, Air Marshal Hill ordered the deployment of the guns to the South Coast. The move of the guns started on the morning of 14 July, was completed on 17 July, and brought speedy results. Between 6 July and 13 July the combined defences brought down 57% of the flying bombs observed.† On 28 August, of the 94 flying bombs approaching the English coast that day 90 were destroyed by barrage balloons, fighters and gun-fire, and of these no less than 65 were shot down by the guns using proximity fuses.

In early August Ed Salant, who always had to be in the thick of the battle, and who had already left for England to make sure that the most efficient use was being made of the VT fuse, sent for me to take over a pilot model of a modification of the fuse that was better suited for use against the flying bomb. This modification involved only a small change

---

* Basil Collier, *The Defence of the United Kingdom,* p 372 (HMSO, London, 1957).
† *Ibid,* pp 380 and 381.

of one or two components in the "potted" green plastic fuse unit that comprised the head of the shell. Thanks mainly to the good offices of Barbara Caldon of OSRD, arrangements were made for Bill Hinman and me to travel together with the unit. So on 16 August we took off from Baltimore Harbor on a Pan-American flying clipper carrying a modified fuse unit. We landed in Newfoundland and that evening took off for our next stop, the River Shannon. Take-off was an interesting experience. The lumbering flying boat rose from a lake and we seemed to be barely skimming over the tops of the fir trees on the eastern shore of the lake, rising and falling in a most precarious manner. Over the Atlantic we were served a magnificent dinner sitting at tables in the forward cabin. I was facing west and I remember seeing the most glorious sunset through the port-hole as we ate a dessert of peaches and ice cream. After dinner we went aft, got into our pyjamas and settled down for a good night's sleep in a comfortable bunk. There was comfortable travel—even in war time! Next morning we put down on the River Shannon; at Shannon Airport we boarded an aircraft with completely opaque windows for the remainder of the trip to England.

I have only recently discovered by checking my passport of that period that we landed at Bristol that evening, 17 August 1944. At the time I had no idea where I was. All I knew was that I was met by Ed Salant who was anxious to get possession of the modified fuse unit, and that we drove off to heaven knows where in an American Army jeep with a very friendly black driver who could hardly be seen in the black-out. I had the vague impression that we were being driven along all-too-narrow country roads in a driverless jeep.

What happened in the next two days is still a blur. Somehow I had arrived in England with a vicious viral infection. About two days later General Pile arranged for me to go down to Folkestone to see the guns in action. He put an old Humber car at my disposal with a WRAC driver who seemed to think that 80 miles per hour was a minimum speed limit. Half-way to Folkestone I remember being laid out on the side of the road with one of the worst nose bleeds I have ever had. We arrived in Folkestone only to find that it was an off day for flying bombs and none came over. I do however remember the great variety of guns lined up along the beaches including one Bofors gun "manned", believe it or not, by a young man and his girl friend in swimming suits!

We returned to London and I stayed on for three weeks and spent some time with Allen Astin and Bill Hinman in connection with bomb and rocket proximity fuses. I recollect staying at the Mount Royal because a V-1 got through one night and exploded nearby. I also visited my parents who were living in a flat in Bramham Gardens, near Gloucester Road. My father's health had seriously deteriorated after working for five years in the City of London under war-time conditions and he had contracted tuberculosis. They too had rented a small cottage on Chinnor Hill where he could join my mother for week-ends, but she had come back to London to look after him, a move that greatly concerned me, knowing as I did of the imminence of the V-1 and V-2 attacks. I could say nothing, however, except to suggest that they stay on in Chinnor for a while; but I could not give them any reason why.

By the middle of September 1944 the capture of their main launching sites on the Continent, and our own counter-measures, had enabled us to contain the attack of the flying bombs. According to Winston Churchill about 8000 in all had been launched against this country, of which some 2400 had got through. Between them they had killed over 6000 people in and around London and seriously injured some 18,000 more. How many people in London owed their lives to the proximity fuses can never be assessed; but there must be hundreds, perhaps thousands, of unknown people still alive today who should be grateful to Ed Salant and to Merle Tuve and his team in the Applied Physics Laboratory of the Johns Hopkins University.

There followed the V-2 rockets, the first of which fell on London on 8 September, one of them on a factory near Kew Gardens. But I was not professionally concerned and now had no reason not to return to my post in the States. Alexander King had wanted to bring his wife and their daughters over to Washington and it was arranged that I should escort them. Accordingly we were all booked out of Gourock on 13 September, sailing on the old four-funnelled Cunarder, the *Aquitania*. We sailed after dark and we thought we were heading south; but next day found us steaming north of Ireland. Ship's rumour had it that a wolf-pack of U-boats was gathered in the south-western approaches to St George's Channel and the Irish Sea. Be that as it may, we had a very pleasant and relaxing seven days enlivened by the presence of the young King daughters, the oldest of whom was then about ten years old. The remainder of the passengers were British and American officers and British wives and families going to join husbands who were already there. We arrived in New York on 21 September. The mood was considerably more optimistic than it had been when we crossed almost exactly one year earlier on the *Queen Mary*. The war had been taken to the continent of Europe and we could believe that the end was in sight.

The remainder of my time in Washington was professionally rather dull compared with the period of intense action in preparation for the flying bombs. On the domestic side, however, we had our excitements: our son Peter was born on 18 January 1945, and was duly registered at the British Embassy in order to preserve his prerogative to be Prime Minister of England or President of the United States.

Germany surrendered in May and Japan in August 1945, but right until August the flow of business through BSCO was considerable, although at no time was any of it, so far as I was concerned, to do with the atom bomb. Alex King has stated* that James Chadwick had an office in BSCO and I occasionally ran into him but never discussed "nuclear" matters with him except for that security lapse that I mentioned earlier. I myself felt out of sympathy with the dropping of atom bombs on Japan. The so-called warnings were in terms of heavy bombing; the time chosen for the dropping of the bombs in the morning rush hour was extremely harsh; and it seemed that if one bomb was necessary, two were not. On the other hand I would in no way have been in favour of Allied landings accompanied by heavy loss of life on both sides. I felt that given the Japanese signals about the possibility of surrender at the time of the Potsdam Conference, one bomb could have been dropped as a demonstration on an area having the lowest population density that could be found in Japan, at a time when people would be indoors and shielded from burns, although not from blast, and the second bomb should have been held in reserve as a substitute, if needed, for an Allied invasion. Bombing is a brutal concomitant of war. The incendiary and high-explosive bomb attacks on the City and the East-end Docks of London growing, in crescendo, to the fire-tornado of Hamburg and the heavy raids on Tokyo were bad enough. But in

---

The Observer, 30 December 1979 (article by John St Jorré and Peter Deeley).

addition to blast and fire, the atom bomb adds two more dimensions, namely that of prompt nuclear radiation around the target with its long-term biological effects and the effects of radioactive fall-out on populations remote from the target and, indeed, in the event of full-scale nuclear warfare, on every living thing on the surface of the globe.

That my time in the United States was very fully occupied with *non-nuclear* matters can perhaps be exemplified by the following extracts from four letters that I received between June 1944 and April 1946: it is convenient to group them here, though the last letter was not written until after my return to England.

From Dr F A Vick of the Ministry of Supply, dated 24 June 1944:

> I should like to take this opportunity of saying how very much A.D.R.D.E. and I value the information you send so quickly and so fully about Section 'T' activities. Such information at once influences the work over here, and our liaison on this subject is better than any other within my experience. The samples you have sent also have been most helpful.

From Professor Sydney Chapman, FRS, Deputy Scientific Adviser to the Army Council, dated 23 January 1945:

> I should like to thank you very much for the great and successful efforts you have made to keep us here up-to-date on the American scientific and technical developments within your wide range of work, and I have no doubt that my successor will be equally appreciative.

From Dr J W Fox, the Government Chemist, dated 28 July 1945:

> I am most grateful that you have continued to provide us with information. Rest assured that it is most helpful and most appreciated. Indeed, were it not largely due to you, we should feel right out of the picture as far as the Japanese war is concerned.

From General Sir Frederick Pile, dated 12 April 1946:

> I was very interested in the booklet 'Flying Bombs'. It is extremely well got up, and there is only one other picture that I would like to see in it; that of the flying bombs tumbling out of the sky on the South coast, when on many occasions there were several being blown up at the same second, thanks to you scientists.

General Pile pays a well-earned and generous tribute to Ed Salant as one of several "supreme experts ... of the U.S.A. forces" without whose help the problems raised by the "new American equipments ... could never have been solved".*

It was in September 1945 that I was able to wind up my affairs in Washington and come back to resume active work as a lecturer at the Imperial College—an appointment which I had held throughout the war, although it had been on a nominal basis during my absence in America. I returned by sea, by RMS *Queen Elizabeth,* which this time travelled by the most direct route, with neither zig nor zag. It was a journey that had a special attraction for me, as for the last two years it had provided me with the only opportunity of a vacation. We docked at Southampton on 29 September 1945. I resumed my teaching in October.

I emphasize these dates because according to Andrew Boyle† it was about this time "not long after the surrender of Japan", that "Basil", his "gifted physicist", entered the Washington scene, just as I was leaving it, "to complicate the already involved and troubled life of Donald Maclean". What a pity I could not have met "Basil" if he really existed—which I doubt—because, having spent the last two years in the manner described by the above four extracts from letters, I could have learned something about the war-time developments in nuclear physics, about which I was ignorant. Fortunately, however, this deficiency was remedied when in late August we visited the home in Princeton of another close war-time colleague and friend in the Department of the Army, Professor H Marston Morse of the Institute for Advanced

---

*General Sir Frederick Pile, ibid., p 338.
†Andrew Boyle, *The Climate of Treason: Five Who Spied for Russia* (p 295)

Studies. Louise Morse had invited Professor Henry DeWolf Smyth of the Department of Physics at Princeton University to dinner. Later Professor Smyth kindly sent me a copy of his report "Atomic Energy for Military Purposes". This was autographed with the date October 1945, so I cannot have received it until after my return to Imperial College. "Atomic Energy" was probably used for the first time publicly in the title of this Report for "Nuclear Energy", I have heard that this was done because of General Leslie Groves's sensitivity to the latter term for reasons of security. If this is so it is surprising that so much other information was given *inside* the Report.

Before leaving Washington in September 1945 I did have the pleasure of being able to nominate Ed Salant for the award of the OBE, which he subsequently received. I am told that when he joined the staff of the Brookhaven National Laboratory after the war this acronym was affectionately interpreted as referring to that "Old Bastard Eddie". I was also told that the British Army Staff in Washington had put forward my own services for similar recognition, but it was found that the name of a Ministry of Production employee could not appear on a War Office list! But the outcome was appropriate, for it had been Ed Salant who had been the driving force in our informal committee; and Bill Brooks and I could share with him the warm satisfaction of having been instrumental in saving many lives through our work, at a time when loss of life was all too common. It had also been a most rewarding privilege to have worked closely and intimately with such a fine physicist, such a great gentleman, and such a devoted Anglophile; certainly none deserved this honour more richly than the late Professor Edward Salant. On one occasion he said he would work in England if the fuses that were needed could not be produced in the United States: and on another that if he and I stuck our necks out too far he hoped we would land up in the same place!

The commendations I received from our American friends for my sojourn of less than two years in Washington were more than generous.*

I am sure that the award of the Medal of Freedom was based primarily

---

*See letter of 3 May 1946, from Mr D Luke Hopkins to W B Mann, p 151 in Appendix A, and of 8 October 1947, from Colonel R E S Williamson to W B Mann, p 156 in Appendix A.

on the part that we three had played in pushing AA Command to deploy their guns to the south-east coast of England for the second, and successful, phase of the battle against the flying bombs. After all, in those crucial days after D-Day it was as much in the interest of the United States as of the British that that area should be properly protected. However, the citation did read in part: *"A nuclear physicist* [my italics] *who represented in Washington the British Ministry of Supply in connection with research and development of proximity fuses, he did much to further the exchange of scientific information among British and American groups, contributing substantially to the superiority of Allied military equipment."* It may have been an echo of this citation that brought the phrase "British born nuclear physicist" into the growing "Basil" mythology. Certainly a reporter told me in early November 1979 that he had been told by colleagues that the notorious—and nebulous—Fifth Man had been the recipient of the Medal of Freedom.

At the risk of being tiresome, then, I must repeat that although I suppose I could properly be described as a "nuclear physicist" I had effectively done no nuclear physics since leaving Berkeley in 1938. It is true that I had been a member of the M.A.U.D. Committee in 1941, but my involvement in its work was minimal. There was no nuclear work whatever involved in the development of the proximity fuses, nor were the "British and American groups" involved in the "exchange of scientific information" concerned with nuclear weaponry.

4

Mainly in Canada

Like so many thousands of men in my position I was delighted to return at the end of the war to what passed for normalcy. In the autumn of 1945 I resumed my teaching at the Imperial College. Our flat in Belvedere Court in Putney was still let, so I in turn rented a room from friends who lived further along the same Upper Richmond Road. G P Thomson was back in harness too and we occasionally played squash together, a game I had not played since 1938 in Berkeley; there my partner had often been Professor Leonard B Loeb, whom I had later come across in Washington in the uniform of a U.S. Navy Captain.

In addition to my lectures, I was again in charge of the third-year physics laboratory, but my principal task was to complete the assembly of the Imperial College Van de Graaff accelerator that we had started to build in the autumn of 1939, but which had been interrupted in 1941. As soon as hostilities with Germany ceased, Mr. Davis and his colleagues in the physics workshop had started construction of the few remaining components, using designs that had been developed for them by J W Boag and P Howard Flanders at the Hammersmith Hospital, London. Work on the accelerator made good progress and in less than a year a voltage of 2.2 million had been achieved. A paper describing the instrument was published in 1948[2]*; in a brief history of the project this

*Superscript numbers refer to References at the end of the book (pp 136).

paper also happens to provide contemporary confirmation of my whereabouts between 1939 and 1946 (see also pp 11 and 14).

Soon after my return to the Imperial College I became interested in continuing the kind of work in which I had engaged between 1936 and 1938 in Ernest Lawrence's laboratory. Thus, on 2 November 1945 I wrote to Professor J D Cockcroft expressing such an interest. (This letter happens to carry the Ministry of Production letter-head; I was already working at the Imperial College, but it may be that my official transfer had not yet taken place.) In his reply he suggested to me that there might be a place for me in the radioactive-tracer work at the Canadian National Research Council's laboratory, then in Montreal, but later to move to Chalk River in Ontario, where he became the first Director.*

G P Thomson who was sympathetic with my desire for more scope also suggested that I submit an application for consideration for his old Chair of Natural Philosophy at the University of Aberdeen. This I did, realizing that if I were successful I would be in a better position to follow my own research interests. I survived a first meeting with the Selection Sub-committee, and was invited to appear before the whole University Court on 30 April 1946.

Negotiations about the Canadian project were also dragging along pretty slowly. I seemed to have about one exchange of correspondence a month with the new Directorate of Atomic Energy, a branch of the Ministry of Supply that had taken over the responsibilities of the Tube Alloys Directorate of the Department of Scientific and Industrial Research. Finally, on 24 April, I was offered a post in the Civil Service as Principal Scientific Officer, with the prospect of working at the Canadian atomic-energy project. The offer was intended to be on permanent establishment, but by some quirk it was found that the salary promised to me could only be paid if my Civil Service status were temporary. After accepting this offer, I immediately wrote to Aberdeen to withdraw my name from their lists; I had already intimated to them, through G P Thomson that I had other possibilities in view.

It was agreed that I should leave for Canada at the end of July 1946. I

*See letters from W B Mann to Professor J D Cockcroft, 2 November 1945, p 149 , and from Professor J D Cockcroft to W B Mann, 19 November 1945, p 150 , in Appendix A.

had however been invited by Sir Alfred Egerton, Secretary of the Royal Society, to give a paper on "Academic Co-operation in the British Empire" at the Royal Society Empire Scientific Conference to be held in June and July 1946. Sir Alfred also asked me to act as recorder of the Steering Group of which he was chairman. The steering Group was to meet on 20 June at the home of the Royal Society, in Burlington House; the title of its assignment was a long one, namely the "Discussion of Methods of Improving the Interchange of Scientists throughout the Empire, including a Discussion on the Future of Scientific Liaison Offices that have been Established during the War"! The other members of the Steering Group were Dr D M Blair, Sir Juan Ghosh, Dr C J Mackenzie, Dr E Marsden, Sir David Rivett, Dr J Smeath-Thomas, Mr F E V Smith and Sir Henry Tizard. We duly met and approved a report and the fact that I was present in the Royal Society on that morning of 20 June is recorded in the Report of the Conference.[6]

In July 1946 I also wrote the preface for the completed 1944-5 Volume X of *Reports on Progress in Physics;* then, on the nineteenth day of that month, I again boarded the *Queen Mary*, this time in Southampton, and set out for Halifax, Nova Scotia, where we docked on the twenty-third. I was bound for the National Research Council of Canada Atomic Energy Project laboratories which had recently completed their move to Chalk River, and I set forth on the first stage of the journey by train from Halifax to Montreal. On arrival in Montral the next day I collapsed and was rushed to the Montreal General Hospital with "no pulse". I later learned that it had been reported to the administrative officer in Chalk River that I had had a heart attack. I hadn't; but I nearly did two days later when I learned the price of my hospital room, after leaving the United Kingdom with the maximum allowance of £10. I recovered quickly—possibly it had been some kind of food poisoning—and finally reached Chalk River on 27 July 1946. After my arrival there I received a letter from a friend at The Institute for Advanced Study, Princeton, asking if I might be interested in an associate professorship in physics at Kenyon College, Ohio, but by now our course for the immediate future had been set.

After a few days break collecting Miriam, Kris and Peter from the home of her cousins Professor and Mrs Walter Colby in Ann Arbor, Michigan, we found temporary residence in an apartment in the pleasant NRC "company town" of Deep River on the bank of the Ottawa River. Across the river, which was there about one-mile wide, was Mt Martin in Quebec, a favourite spot for skiing in winter, which was easily accessible on skiis when the ice on the Ottawa River attained a thickness of one or two feet.

Our family reunion was not, however, destined to last long. Before leaving the United Kingdom I had been approached with regard to taking a position as assistant to the principal U.K. Scientific Adviser on the United Nations Atomic Energy Commission. I declined this, however, as it seemed to be a committee and paper-work job and I felt I had shovelled enough paper back and forth during the six years of the war. But on 10 August Dr Cockcroft received an "immediate" cable from the Ministry of Supply in London that requested my presence at the U.K. Delegation to the United Nations in New York on 12 August.* Fortunately, as is so often the case, the initial urgency became less pressing and I flew down to New York on 15 August. There, apparently‡, the fort was being held by Dr William Penney, my old friend and contemporary from the Imperial College who used to help me to understand the finer nuances of mathematics in return for some practical co-operation on the more tedious and routine experiments of the second-year physics laboratory. Now he was devising brilliantly simple real-world experiments that gave incisive and well-defined results in contrast to less successful experiments requiring complicated and elaborate equipment.

Bill Penney stayed on for a few days and on 19 August we were invited to Bernard Baruch's 76th birthday party at his home and estate on Long Island. There I met Clare Booth Luce, Eugene Black and Andrei Gromyko before lunch, at which I sat next to Henry Luce. I had some apprehensions about my table companion as I thought our political views might not exactly coincide, but I found him to be most pleasant and congenial.

From the point of view of creature comfort I have never, before or since, been treated so well by any of the governments, U.K., Canadian or U.S., by which I have been employed. I had inherited a pleasant office

---

*Cable of 10 August 1946 from F How to J D Cockcroft, p 151 in Appendix A.
‡Letter of 16 August 1946 to Dr J D Cockcroft from W B Mann, p 152 in Appendix A.

with a spacious wooden desk and a most affable and efficient secretary, Jean Birney, from Canada. There was also included a Lincoln sedan with electrically operated windows (at that time, an unusual refinement), and a driver who took me home at night and picked me up in the morning. I felt quite embarrassed by such luxury. When I arrived at the British Embassy in Washington two years later it was with great pleasure that I found that Jean Birney had preceded me there.

The UN Atomic Energy Commission had established a number of committees to advise on the various problems concerned with the control of atomic energy. First there was a Working Committee, comprised of one representative from each nation represented on the Commission, whose function was to consider proposals made at sessions of the Commission, and after consideration to report back its recommendations. To help it the Working Committee established three other committees, namely: (i) Committee 2, to examine questions associated with the control of atomic energy activities and to make specific recommendations for such control; (ii) a Legal Advisory Committee, to examine the legal aspects of the relationships between the systems or measures of control as recommended by Committee 2, and to draft a treaty or treaties for the Working Committee; and (iii) a Scientific and Technical Committee, to advise on the scientific aspects of the problem.

On 31 July 1946 Committee 2 had requested the Scientific and Technical Committee "to prepare a report on the question of whether effective control of atomic energy is possible, together with an indication of the methods by which the Scientific and Technical Committee considers that effective control can be achieved".

When I arrived in New York a fortnight later I found that I was to take over for G P Thomson as the U.K. representative on this Scientific and Technical Committee. It had already done much towards the completion of its report, but it had still to obtain final agreement between the nations represented.

Professor H A Kramers was chairman of the Committee. Its other members were the representatives of Australia, Brazil, Canada, China, Egypt, France, Mexico, Poland, the U.S.S.R., the U.K. and U.S.A.* Dr

*See Plate III.

Franklin S Cooper, ably assisted by Miss Margaret Croake, headed the group from the UN Secretariat that aided the Committee in the preparation of its Report.

The deliberations of the Committee were time-consuming and tedious. There was no simultaneous translation in those days and on occasion the representative of the U.S.S.R. would make hour-long statements in Russian. I started to smoke cigarettes to keep awake. At the end of each day, I had to summarize the proceedings in a cable to the Foreign Office. One day I concluded the cable by saying that "Skobeltsin played out time on a sticky wicket." A day or two later Mr V G Lawford, private secretary to Sir Alexander Cadogan, who was then United Kingdom ambassador to the United Nations, remarked to me that my cables were perhaps somewhat flippant; had I seen the distribution of that particular series? I said that I had not, so he sent it to me. The first listed recipient was HM the King, the second his Prime Minister, the third the Foreign Secretary, and so on down the line! Thereafter I restrained my attempts at humour.

However, I came to have a great respect for Sir Alexander's team. Most of them conservative to the core, from the proper schools and universities, they were loyal to a man to the Labour Secretary of State for Foreign Affairs, Ernest Bevin. When he came over for a UN session they were working day and night to make sure that "the SS" had the very best that they could give. One of the team, Richard Miles, was assigned to guide me through the intricacies of Foreign Office and diplomatic etiquette. He was a wonderful guide and we worked well together. I was equally grateful to Colonel Cosmo Nevill, a British officer assigned to the UN Military Staff Committee. He and Mrs Nevill took me under their wing, and we still drink port out of the glasses they gave us when they visited us later in Deep River.

On this occasion I spent about seven weeks in New York. The introduction to the Scientific and Technical Committee's Report notes that there were "eight weeks of intensive study and discussion of the problem" in informal meetings of the committee. About half-way through that period, however, we thought that we had reached agreement on a draft report and we arranged a second formal meeting of the committee for 3 September to approve it.

On 29 August John Cockcroft had asked if I could return as soon as possible to Chalk River as Dr W Mayneord, the well-known medical physicist, was visiting during the week of 1 September and especially wished to see me. I felt, however, that I must stay over in New York until after the meeting on the third, especially as Sir Alexander Cadogan, clearly expecting the final vote to be a formal matter, had appointed me, from 31 August, as his scientific adviser and alternate delegate both on the UN Atomic Energy Commission and on its committees.* So I missed a pleasant autumn week-end in Deep River — only to discover on Monday 2 September that the U.S.S.R. delegation was not in a position to approve the report.

I must have returned to Deep River for a few days thereafter, and between meetings, because my passport shows that I again entered the United States through the airport at Massena, New York, on 17 September 1946. After more informal discussions the second formal meeting of the committee to approve our report, was rearranged for 26 September.

A few days before this meeting took place I received a note from G P Thomson to say that he expected to be back to relieve me on 26 September,† but he did not arrive in time for the meeting, and I had the privilege of delivering the vote for the United Kingdom. There was still considerable doubt which way the U.S.S.R. delegate would vote. I was seated between Professor S P Alexandrov (U.S.S.R.) and Professor R C Tolman (U.S.A.) and I was so surprised when the former voted in favour of the report that it took me a moment to collect myself in order to signify our own vote in favour. I believe that this was the only vote in the Commission or its committees that ever was unanimous.

The Report[6] itself was pretty innocuous and certainly not worth the time that we spent on it because it scarcely opened the way to the "effective control of atomic energy". It has, however, a retrospective interest, in that it was the first report to illustrate pictorially the various stages in the production of atomic energy and the uses of radioactive materials in hospitals and laboratories. This chart also identified those

*Letter of 31 August 1946 from Sir Alexander Cadogan to Mr Trygve Lie, p 152 in Appendix A.
†Letter of 16 September 1946, from Sir George Thomson to W B Mann, p 153 in Appendix A.

stages where there could be "possible diversion to secret weapons production".

A few days after this meeting, at the end of September or the beginning of October 1946, I returned to Canada. At Chalk River I was attached to the Medical and Biological Research Branch headed by André J Cipriani, MD, and was assigned the task of starting a group that would be responsible for producing radioactivity standards for the assay of radioactive materials for medical and biological applications.

During my absence in New York Miriam and the children had moved into a comfortable prefabricated three-bedroom, semi-detached house on Parkdale Avenue in Deep River. During the winters ahead temperatures were to drop as low as –40°C (or Fahrenheit!), and it is interesting to reflect that the house was so well insulated that we could keep comfortably warm in winter by feeding about two scuttles of coal a day to a furnace in the basement. There was no habitation between us and the north pole: by day the winter skies were mostly blue and clear, we saw the *aurora borealis* on summer evenings, the bears often turned our garbage cans over at night, and the black flies drove us nearly crazy in June. But, above all, the life was wonderful and we made many friends.

For the next two and a half months I was able to concentrate on the task of setting up a radioactivity-standards laboratory. During my absence in New York John Cockcroft had left Chalk River to become Director of the U.K. Atomic Energy Research Establishment at Harwell and Dr W Bennett Lewis had been appointed Director of Research at Chalk River. In 1947 Professor David A Keys of McGill University was appointed National Research Council Vice-President in charge of the Chalk River Atomic Energy Project.

Although I had written to G P Thomson as early as 26 August 1946, asking him if he could raise the question of the appointment of a permanent scientific assistant adviser before he left London, as my family and my work needed me in Canada, my sojourn there was again to be interrupted. G P wrote on 19 November from New York to say that I might "be asked to come south again" somewhere around 4 and 5 December as he was planning to take a few days off before his departure for the U.K. on 12 December. He concluded: "Things are working up here and you may have quite an interesting time. We have been told to make a report by the end of the year which means that Committee 2 must do it by December 20th. This will no doubt be only an interim report but it is quite possible that fundamental issues might have to be faced in it." This was followed a week later by another letter from G P* from which I was relieved to learn that Sir James Chadwick would be coming to take over on a permanent basis in the New Year. G P's optimistic statement that the only difference would be the amount of clothes I packed struck me as being something of an understatement in that my short-term comings and extended goings were considerably upsetting André Cipriani's plans for the work on which we were engaged.

I could not of course evade G P's request. My passport shows that I entered the United States through the airport at Burlington, Vermont, on 8 December. I am not sure whether I overlapped with G P, but I do remember that Richard Miles and I were given the assignment of preparing a speech for Alexander Cadogan to give to the next session of the Atomic Energy Commission.

During my five months in New York and Deep River I had become acquainted with George Laurence, the Scientific Adviser to General A G L MacNaughton, the head of the Canadian delegation. I was therefore glad to find that the National Research Council travel office at Chalk River had booked me into the Biltmore Hotel in close proximity to the Canadians. General MacNaughton frequently held "open house" in the evening in his suite for members of his delegation, and I was invited to join them on two or three occasions. The General was a most delightful and kindly host, who was at the time President of the Canadian Atomic Energy Control Board. George Laurence and George Ignatieff too were usually present and these evenings were both stimulating and helpful.

In October the U.K. Security Council and Atomic Energy Commission Delegations had moved from Exchange Place to the 61st floor of the Empire State Building. The U.S. Delegation was on the next floor and it was pleasant to be able to talk to my old friend from Berkeley days, Robert Oppenheimer who often visited there. He was at that time

---

*Letter of 26 November 1946, from Sir George Thomson to W B Mann, p 154 in Appendix A.

already deeply concerned with the question of "overkill" by atomic weapons.

One odd incident is still impressed on my memory. On either 12 or 13 December I was strolling back to the Empire State Building along 47th Street at about noon. Suddenly I received an excruciatingly painful eyeful of dirt. I hurried up to the 60th floor wash-room and sluiced my eye out with water. Next morning I read in the *Herald Tribune* that at mid-day before, Captain Eddie Rickenbacker had scattered Damon Runyon's ashes over Times Square. At least, I felt, I might have been among his residuary legatees.

The meeting to which I have referred above was due to take place just before Christmas, so Richard and I had less than a fortnight to brief Sir Alexander on his response to the Baruch proposals, based on the Acheson — Lilienthal Report, which were to be the main item of business. I had looked through the U.S. proposals and noted that in addition to the Atomic Development Authority (ADA), they made reference to something like "national bodies for the control of atomic energy". I found this disturbing because the U.S.S.R. Delegation was continuously maintaining that international control was unnecessary and that national control would suffice. So I told Richard that I would go and ask Paul Fine in the U.S. Delegation about this.

However when I reached their offices I ran not only into Paul Fine but also into Bernard Baruch himself who greeted me with his usual warm cordiality. I explained my concern, but the problem was swept aside by Baruch's tremendous enthusiasm for his proposals. "They're a Christmas present to the world", he told me; "A Mother Hubbard that defines the boundaries without revealing the details." I must have looked completely lost because he repeated the second part of the statement. I also noticed that Paul Fine alongside me was trying to say something, but I could not listen to him and the great man too. So I bade farewell and departed in what felt more like a rout than a dignified exit.

Richard Miles was waiting to learn what I had gleaned from my mission. I told him that I had run into Bernard Baruch and that I could not imagine what he was talking about; all I knew about Mother Hubbard was that *her* cupboard was bare. Richard could not help me, so I telephoned Paul. He had indeed been trying to explain to me that a Mother Hubbard was a maternity smock.

Richard and I worked for the rest of the day on Cadogan's speech and then repaired to his hotel to await for him to come back from a Security Council meeting at Lake Success. It was not until his return at 2 o'clock the next morning that I was able to tell Cadogan about my encounter with Baruch. Yes, Baruch had told him that his proposals were a Mother Hubbard, but he did not understand what he meant. I was at least able to resolve that problem. We went through the speech together which fortunately he accepted, and we then turned in to get some sleep before the meeting of the Commission later that morning.

We drove out to Lake Success together and in the car I raised with Sir Alexander a matter that had been bothering me, and that was the role of scientists in diplomacy and government, about which there was at that time considerable discussion. Some scientists, especially in the United States, believed that because they had released the ultimate source of power, and because they were moral people who believed in peace, they should govern or have a very big share in government. Others felt (perhaps with some justification) that scientists, by and large, were politically illiterate and should have no part whatsoever in government. My view was that scientists should not *ipso facto* "govern the world" but that, equally, just because they were scientists they should not be automatically *excluded* from government.

I had heard that G P Thomson had received a memorandum informing him that his advice should be limited to scientific matters and should not extend to questions of policy. I was uneasily aware that Sir Alexander must have noticed that during my time with the U.K. delegation I had definitely stuck my nose into policy matters — both with our own people and in discussion with members of other delegations. I knew too that I had contributed substantially to the speech he was going to make. This then was an opportunity for me to make my excuses. I told him that I had perhaps exceeded my functions as his scientific adviser and trespassed into territory that should have been left to the politicians. First of all he courteously and gently reproved me by saying that he considered himself to be a statesman and *not* a politician. But then he generously added that we were a small team and we all had to pull our weight. The matter was closed but in a most heart-warming way. He was *indeed* a statesman.

I remember little of the meeting at Lake Success. It took place around the horse-shoe table of the Security Council. Colonel Hodgson represented Australia, General MacNaughton represented Canada, Mr Baruch the U.S.A. and Mr Gromyko the U.S.S.R. There was, however, no consensus whatsoever on the control of atomic energy. The U.S. proposed the creation of "an International Atomic Development Authority for the international control of dangerous activities involved in the peaceful uses of atomic energy". The U.S.S.R. proposal was "to conclude an international convention for outlawing production and application of weapons based upon the use of atomic energy for the purpose of mass destruction". So, there between the two poles the debate ended.

My passport shows that I returned by air to Dorval, PQ, on 22 December 1946. I was accompanied by George H Briggs, the Scientific Adviser to the Australian Delegation. We enjoyed a very pleasant white Christmas together with the family in Deep River.

I returned briefly to New York in late January 1947, but upon arrival I found that my journey had been unnecessary.* Nevertheless, it was opportune in that I was able to welcome and brief Sir James Chadwick† who arrived on 31 January. When he came into the office I offered him my chair at the desk, but he courteously took one of the other chairs with words to the effect that as long as I was there I was in charge. He had not had a very good crossing on the *Queen Mary* and was not feeling well. He asked if I had heard from the Foreign Office to whom he had suggested a five-day overlap. I replied that I had not, but had allowed for two days and was planning to return to Canada on Sunday, 2 February. This did not please him at all, but I assured him that little was happening at that time. After telling me something about his visits to Denmark, to see Professor and Mrs Bohr, and to Sweden immediately after the war he went back to his hotel to rest. This was probably the last time I saw him but I did receive a letter from him about a month later telling me that Sir Charles Darwin was now filling the Adviser's job in New York and thanking me for some information about the availability of polonium.‡

---

*Letter of 3 February 1947 from Sir Alexander Cadogan to W B Mann, p 154 in Appendix A.

†Letter of 26 November 1946 from Sir George Thomson to W B Mann, p 154 in Appendix A.

‡Letter of 2 March 1947, from Sir James Chadwick to W B Mann, p 155 in Appendix A.

He had also explained my position to Sir Alexander Cadogan who agreed that I would not be called back to New York unless it was really necessary.

I did however comply with Cadogan's request in his letter of 3 February for some reflections on my sojourn in New York. I sent a short memorandum to Richard Miles on the subject of atomic-energy control and concomitant inspection requirements, with a list of facilities that would require inspection and the numbers and kind of personnel required to effect it. It was very much of an instructed guess but Richard told me that a copy had been forwarded to the Cabinet Advisory Committee on Atomic Energy.

In August 1947 I made one more trip to New York at G P Thomson's request. All I remember of it now is going to see the U.K. Delegation travel officer in order to make arrangements for my return journey to Chalk River. I sat on the radiator in front of the window alongside his desk and, leaning back, I suddenly realized that I was leaning into empty space. Taking hold of the window sill I gingerly drew myself forward until my feet rested once more on the floor. It so happened that the windows had been washed and as the top and bottom halves of the window overlapped exactly it was very easy to make the mistake of thinking that they were both shut. I pointed out that it would be much safer if it were impossible to raise the bottom part so far, because one would then see two horizontal bars instead of one dividing the upper and lower parts of the window. I hope something was done about this before anyone leaned further back than I. It is possible, however, that the windows were opened on the 61st floor only to humour the preference of the British for "fresh air" rather than air-conditioning.

This visit marked the end of my association with the work of the United Nations in New York and at Lake Success. I had been in the United States for some six or seven weeks from 15 August 1946 (with a short break of a few days back in Canada in mid-September): and again for a fortnight from 8 December to 22 December. Brief visits followed in late January 1947, when I was able to hand over to Sir James Chadwick, and again in August of the same year. My only other visits to the United States were not concerned with United Nations' business. As mentioned earlier (p 45), I went to Ann Arbor, Michigan, for a few days in July 1946, soon after my arrival in Canada, to bring Miriam and the children to Deep River. Then in April 1948 (see p 58) we went to the Washington meeting of the American Physical Society, and we visited friends in Arlington, Virginia, and in Washington, and the Marston Morses in Princeton on our return journey to Canada in the first week in May.

We also made a week-end sight-seeing and shopping excursion in October 1947, a short distance across the border by car to Tupper Lake, acccompanied by our Deep River friends Charles and Jean Ford and Agnes Comisky. As a souvenir of that trip we are still using the Sunbeam Mixmaster that we purchased!

If I have chronicled these visits to the United States fairly fully it is because of Andrew Boyle's suggestion (already referred to on p 40) that the mysterious "Basil" entered the Washington scene in late 1945 and that "until October 1948 the British scientist ['Basil'] continued to see Donald Maclean as regularly as ever".* The official and other assignments that I have detailed above are confirmed not only by the letters appended to this book, the originals of which have been made available for verification, but also by many more letters in my files which fill in the gaps — some of them with outspoken but confidential comments by members of the various delegations about other delegations. When Professor Weinstein states that "Dr Mann has produced his passport and other personal records to show that he left the United States in September 1945, returning only in late December 1948, months after Maclean's departure"†, it must be clear that he is not referring to the visits of limited duration which I have here recorded.

Most of my visits to New York City were concentrated in the period from 15 August 1946, to 22 December of the same year. Prior to that, apart from the few days in Ann Arbor, I had been in the United Kingdom since September 1945. I returned to New York for very short visits in January and August 1947, having spent a month going to and returning from London in June and July 1947 (see p 58). We spent a week or ten days on a trip to Washington with a visit to Princeton on the way back to Canada in April and May 1948.

The infrequency of my visits to the United States after 1946 — only

---

*Andrew Boyle, *The Climate of Treason: Five Who Spied for Russia*, pp 295 and 311.
†Allen Weinstein, *Spy Hunt* in *The Washington Post* of 25 January 1980, paraphrased in part on pp 132 and 133.

three short ones in 1947, and one in 1948 — combined on the other hand with long periods when my whereabouts outside the U.S. can be documented by my letters, publications and passport entries, forms no basis at all for drawing any correlation between my activities from September 1945 to December 1948 and those of Andrew Boyle's nebulous "Basil", who during approximately the same period continued to see Maclean as *regularly as ever* ("advising which nuclear-programme files, and which items in those files should be extracted from the U.S. Atomic Energy Commission's headquarters"*).

As far as Wilfrid Mann was concerned — to return to reality — my stints of duty in New York and at Lake Success had been interesting and full of hard work. But in retrospect they had yielded little, and my first year of work at Chalk River had been disastrously fragmented. A couple of extracts from letters that I received later may serve as an epilogue to this interlude in my career and as an ironic prelude to the thirty years of world history that have since elapsed. On 14 April 1948 Richard Miles writes: "I am so glad that you are coming down to Washington and New York. I am afraid you will find very little left of the Atomic Energy Commission by then, but we will need to thrash out the whys and wherefores of its failures, and I look forward to joining with you in an inquest. You are probably quite right in suggesting that the Russians want to out-flank us strategically, but ...". Later David Lilienthal wrote: "On July 29, 1949, the United Nations Atomic Energy Commission, after three years barren of results, suspended their deliberations indefinitely"†

For the rest of my time in Canada I was able to work with little interruption, though I had occasion to leave Chalk River a couple of times in June 1947.

On 13 June my name is listed in the programme of a meeting, organized by the Canadian Association of Professional Physicists in London, Ontario, as presenting a paper on electrostatic high-voltage generators. By way of confirmation I still have a copy of the London "Free Press" in which my photograph appears with my friend and colleague from Chalk River, Professor G M Volkoff of the University of British Columbia.

*The Climate of Treason: Five Who Spied for Russia, p 311.
†This I do Believe, by David E Lilienthal, Harper and Brothers, New York, 1949.

Then on 22 June I left by air for England because of the death of my father. He had been seriously ill with tuberculosis since the end of the war and had gone to a sanatorium above Montreaux to try to recover. My mother had had a very rough trip in a small plane to Switzerland to be with him during his last days. As my sister and her husband, Cecilie and Clement Pain, were teaching in Uganda as members of the Church Missionary Society, I left immediately for London to help my mother on her return. I sailed back from England on 16 July on the *Empress of Canada* that reached Quebec City on 22 July 1947. It was with warm appreciation that I learned after my return to Chalk River that I had without even asking for it been granted compassionate leave by my considerate superiors in the Ministry of Supply.

My only other recorded absence from Canada (referred to in Richard Miles's letter quoted above) occurred in 1948 when the whole family drove down to Washington, DC, to stay with friends and for me to attend the Washington meeting of the American Physical Society. My passport shows that we entered the United States at the Thousand Islands Bridge, New York, on 27 April 1948. Bruno and Marianne Pontecorvo left on the same day and we met them in the mountains of Pennsylvania for lunch. In view of the notoriety later associated with Bruno, a brief digression on our acquaintance may not be out of place.

Deep River was largely a self-contained community, and the Pontecorvos were among the wide circle of friends we made there. Bruno himself was a good physicist, one of the best tennis players in the community, an amusing conversationalist, a quite popular local personality, and, as I remember, not given to political views. He and I car-pooled together with John Robson towards the end of my tour in Deep River. None of us was, however, at that time renowned for his early rising, and I fear that the late-arrival book, if still on file, could give an almost daily record of my attendance at the Chalk River laboratory. I remember one day we were a few minutes late but the book had not yet been put out, and Pontecorvo insisted that we wait while it was brought out for us to sign. (By way of mitigation I should also remark that we generally left the laboratory in the evening considerably after the NRC buses had returned to Deep River.)

Certainly none of us had any reason to suspect that Bruno was an agent for the Russians or indeed for any other power. His cosmopolitan background had given him a certain chameleon-like quality which enabled him to feel at home in any environment.

Nor indeed did the Chalk River laboratories seem at that time to provide a promising field for espionage of any kind. They were concerned not with weapons but with reactor design and the peaceful applications of atomic energy. If Pontecorvo had been linked in some way with the United States weapons development, then that would have been another matter; but we cannot remember his leaving Deep River more than very occasionally. If his job was that of a courier, then he was very awkwardly placed in such an outpost of science, 120 miles up the Ottawa River from Ottawa. The information publicly released in the Smyth Report would have enabled any competent scientist in a Soviet laboratory to have deduced just about as much as Pontecorvo could have elicited from the inside. (When, three years later, I was concerned with assessing the Russian potential, I would have given an eye-tooth to have seen the Russian equivalent of the Smyth Report, illustrated as it was with photographs of our production plants.)

It will always remain a mystery at what stage he decided that he ought to make a clean break with his western associates. Certainly his past experiences must have taught him what it was like to be a hunted character. He fled from Italy under Mussolini; he was reputed to have escaped from Paris on a bicycle about half-an-hour ahead of the occupying German forces. I remember that shortly before he left Canada to take up an appointment at the new Atomic Energy Research Establishment at Harwell in Berkshire he discussed at length with me whether to take his old Canadian Ford with him or whether to order a new Standard Vanguard as this was to be a permanent move. (In the end he ordered the Vanguard.) This may have been part of an elaborate ploy — but if so, what was the purpose of it? I am informed by an English friend who knew him in his Harwell days that Bruno had a similar conversation with him about his long-term plans for his children after he had been offered a professorship at Liverpool.

It later emerged that he had had communist connections in the past. If that alone were proof of treachery, there must be men of great integrity in public life today who would scarcely emerge unscathed. (There is an apposite story of a French scientist who was denied a visa to enter the United States because he estimated on his application form that some

30% of his friends were communists. As he had a wide circle of friends right across the board, he had based this figure on the communist share of the poll in the last general election.)

At all events, something happened while he and Marianne Pontecorvo were on that fateful holiday in Italy which determined them to make for Russia. His defection cannot efface from those of us who knew him in Chalk River the memory of a very lively and friendly colleague.

In late June of 1948 John Cockcroft came back to visit Chalk River. He was walking with W B Lewis and me towards the plant gate one afternoon when he suddenly broached a most unexpected subject. The Directorate of Atomic Energy had a representative in Washington DC who cooperated with the CIA on atomic-energy intelligence. The present incumbent, who had an office in CIA headquarters, believed that such liaison was no longer worth while, had apparently expressed as much to his CIA colleagues, and was being recalled in October. Dr Walter F Colby was then currently Director of Intelligence at the Atomic Energy Commission and it was felt that this might help me in salvaging the situation as it was known that we had a close family link as Miriam and Mrs Colby were first cousins.

Once I had got over my surprise, I agreed to undertake this new task which looked as if it could be full of interest. On 13 July I received a letter from Mr J B L Munro, Assistant Secretary for Establishments in the Ministry of Supply, formally offering me the job and asking urgently for a reply by cable. However, I now discovered that before going to Washington in October it would be desirable for me to have a two-month briefing in London. This would have involved our leaving Chalk River immediately which I felt would be unfair to my Canadian colleagues after all my earlier truancies.

In part Munro's letter also read: "A *sine qua non* of the proper handling of this post is the ability to collaborate with Americans, which involves not only strictly official relationships but also a large measure of social intercourse which is essential in this somewhat specialised and ill-defined field. We are assured by . . . Cockcroft that you will have no difficulty on this score." I should have been warned; how little did I realize what lay ahead!

I apparently replied that it would be unreasonable to leave work undone in Chalk River because his next letter, of 6 August read in part: "While we would naturally prefer if you could return before the end of September we agree that you should complete your present work. If this means that you cannot return before the end of September we shall accept the position and make interim arrangements for the Washington post. We would, however, expect you to be ready, after a course of initiation here, to go to Washington at the end of November or beginning of December." After a hectic week of farewells from Deep River we were driven to Chalk River Station on 2 October 1948, by our good friends Dr and Mrs Norval Williamson, the greatly respected surgeon at the Deep River Hospital and his wife. There they saw us off at 12.30 am by the CPR trans-Canada train bound for Montreal. The same morning at 10 am we boarded the *Empress of France* bound for Liverpool.

5
Washington Again

After a very pleasant voyage we disembarked in Liverpool on 9 October 1948. Our London flat had become vacant about that time so we were able to live there for the two months that we stayed in London for my "course of initiation" in the special group concerned with atomic-energy intelligence in the Ministry of Supply's Directorate of Atomic Energy. This special group was headed by a retired lieutenant-commander of the Royal Navy who was seconded part-time from MI6. He had been concerned with atomic-energy intelligence during the war and had worked with our friend Lief Tronstad. Because of his naval antecedents he was commonly known to his friends and colleagues as "the Admiral". He is no longer alive but, while he was, he shunned publicity and I have never seen his name in print in this context. He was, I am sure, a good intelligence officer but so secretive that it was almost impossible for an outsider like myself to judge. In later years he showed considerable concern for my own future and appreciation for what I had done as his representative in the United States.

My course of initiation consisted mainly of reading voluminous files including, after I had received the necessary top-secret-plus clearance, a limited number of decyphered intercepts. There were also briefing sessions with the other members of the special group.

It was pleasant to be home again. The time passed quickly and we were booked to sail on the *Queen Elizabeth* on 16 December 1948. The "Admiral" gave me introductions to a number of colleagues in Washington. They included Geoffrey Paterson and Peter Dwyer, the respective MI5 and MI6 Washington representatives, and Lord Tedder with the British Joint Services Mission. There was also James Angleton of the CIA who had been a pupil at an English public school (not that I considered that to be a disadvantage). I did not however, meet him until later. And then there were three of four colleagues in the nuclear energy group whom it is not necessary to identify, especially as I shall be quoting some of their more outspoken comments made to me in conversations soon after my arrival concerning the subject of U.K. — U.S. co-operation. I have only in the last few months dug up notes of these conversations, buried in a notebook containing unclassified scientific and other notes. Unfortunately, however, the notes are sprinkled lavishly with initials and acronyms. To decipher them after all these years has been a major feat of memory, and there is still one of them that defeats me.

We disembarked from the *Queen Elizabeth* in New York on 21 December, as is duly recorded in both Miriam's passport and my own. We had been fortunate in having as a travelling companion our friend Professor Lansing V Hammond of the Commonwealth Fund, but less fortunate in encountering the edge of a hurricane during which Kris and I witnessed, from the deck where we were standing, waves that were some forty feet in height.

The British Consulate in New York kindly arranged for us to be met and helped on our way to the Pennsylvania Station whence we went by train to Washington. There we were met by Gordon Baines, the "Admiral's" two-month representative *ad interim*, with the news that we had just been turned out of our office in the CIA headquarters building that abutted to and in some way penetrated into the old Senate Brewery near Watergate. (How far it penetrated I cannot remember, but far enough that we could get free beer served at a bar equipped with beer pumps with British pub-style handles that brought beer up from the basement.) Gordon, who not long afterwards emigrated from the U.K. to take up an administrative post with the NRC at Chalk River, had however found temporary quarters for me and an MI6 secretary, Sybil, at the British Embassy. In view of what John Cockcroft had told me back in June, I had expected to find a difficult situation; but this was certainly not a very promising start.

We spent Christmas at the Gralyn Hotel near N Street and Connecticut Avenue, NW. Kris, now six, said that as we didn't have a Christmas tree, we should put the presents under the bed. I cannot remember that we *had* many presents that year; but we did visit kind friends in Virginia, connected with the Department of the Navy, for Christmas dinner.

When I presented myself to my future colleagues at CIA I heard much to depress me. Two of them in separate discussions spoke very frankly. They were themselves cordial and friendly, and they clearly felt it was their job to warn me against expecting too much. They had in fact asked the "Admiral" last autumn if he had warned me of what I was coming to, but he said he had not. The "Admiral" had made a mistake at that time in applying too much pressure to the technical people (ie the AEC). Any falling off of intimacy with the U.S. organizations was due to pressure from without and was not personal. The members of the CIA nuclear-energy group had been warned that it might be unwise to be seen lunching with me in town (even at the Cosmos Club!) for fear of awkward questions being asked. (But we could lunch together at the CIA cafeteria.) They felt that it would take many weeks or months to resolve the situation even if the Combined Policy Committee acted and that the question of taking the matter to the CPC had been under discussion for a year and a half. The Colonel in charge of the nuclear-energy group, was entirely sympathetic to co-operation but had to make the decision to discontinue it in face of the possible death of his own organization. Even a report on heavy water might not be handed to us as the AEC were objecting to our getting their *restricted* technical information. There would be a meeting "tomorrow" to decide this and "the report might come to us with offending passages deleted". On the other hand, if I went home that would mean a cutting off of all British information on the assessment of raw intelligence, about which they hardly dared think.

It was emphasized that a fundamental difficulty was the difference between the Espionage Act and the McMahon Atomic Energy Act of 1946. The former made it an offence to divulge information that would jeopardise the security of the United States, but the latter made it an offence to divulge *any* information relating to the development of nuclear energy.

When I was young I had been given a copy of Hilaire Belloc's *Cautionary Tales for Children* in which there was a young lady named Matilda who called fire when there was none, but later called in vain when a real fire broke out; and another child, an unfortunate boy who had been slowly devoured by a lion because he let go of his nurse's hand. By the time these briefings had finished I felt an affinity with each of these sad characters. I could hardly blame either the "Admiral" or the Colonel for their apprehensions; but it did not make it any easier for me to collaborate with those whose task it was to predict a time-scale for the production of a Russian bomb without some knowledge of the magnitude of the production processes involved.

I did not report all this to the "Admiral". For one thing I did not believe the criticism of him was justified. I probably just went home and took it out on a long-suffering family. But I had the feeling that I was going to be to a large extent on my own in my mission. The special nuclear-energy group in CIA was completely fettered by the restrictions of the McMahon Atomic Energy Act, but was, on the other hand, voraciously eager to receive British raw and processed intelligence reports, and to make theirs available when they did not involve AEC restricted technical information. This great asset was the only thing that made my job tenable.

There was some other compensation in that both Miriam and I found in Peter Dwyer, the MI6 representative in Washington and my nearest contact in the Embassy, a witty and congenial colleague with a good sense of humour. I am sure that it was largely due to him that we did not take the next available ship back home to the United Kingdom.

As the heavy-water report had still not been released to us, I decided to look for technical information on my own initiative. So about ten days after the second of these dreary discussions I hied me off to Trail in British Columbia where the Canadians were producing, I believe, what was then the world supply of heavy water. It was on 15 March 1949, that I re-entered Canada at Paterson, BC. In the next few days I became an instant expert in the electrolytic enrichment of heavy water.

On the way back to Washington I stopped in Sun Valley, Idaho, for four or five days of skiing. On the last day I took the lift up to Mt Baldy and had a pleasant enough descent, taking some lovely photographs with a second-hand war-time Leica camera that I had bought in Washington. In late afternoon I came to the edge of a canyon that was on the downward trail and was puzzled by a muted roar that greeted me as I peered over the edge. It turned out that the afternoon sun had melted the upper layer of snow that had then glazed over as the sun moved on. The noise was that of skiers side-slipping down. There was some kind of international contest taking place later in the week and as I waited and watched the French team swept by more or less with noses to the toes of their skies. I learned afterwards that one of them came out of it with a broken hip. I finally ventured into the canyon; I emerged somewhat bruised and the worse for wear but with my precious camera undamaged.

On 8 May 1949, I flew to the U.K. for discussions, returning to Washington two weeks later. By now I had established a *modus vivendi* with my American colleagues based on the exchange of raw intelligence and the strict avoidance of any matters that came within the purview of the McMahon Act. Sometimes when I sought some special information I would be referred by the CIA to Gordon Arneson, for example at the Department of State, to Walter Colby at the Atomic Energy Commission, to Robert Le Baron at Defence and maybe even back to CIA. Relations with my U.S. colleagues had become very congenial and they no longer appeared to be worried about our being seen together in public. The question of our ever again being granted office space in CIA was, however, never discussed, nor did I myself mention it. Nor did anyone else seem anxious to take Sybil and me under their roof. However, as I had established squatters' rights at the British Embassy in the temporary wing, long since demolished, on the north side of the courtyard, it was eventually decided to convert my "non-person" status into that of an attaché in atomic energy. It was not until just before leaving in 1951 that I learned I was less formally referred to around the embassy as the "atom bomb".

A pleasant interlude occurred in the first week of June 1949 when John Cockcroft visited Washington, and I was fortunate enough to be invited to accompany him to an elegant lunch which Stephen Early, Deputy Secretary of Defense, gave in his honour in the Secretary's dining-room in the Pentagon, overlooking the Potomac River. On the

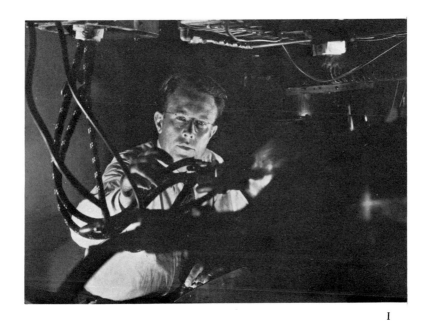

I

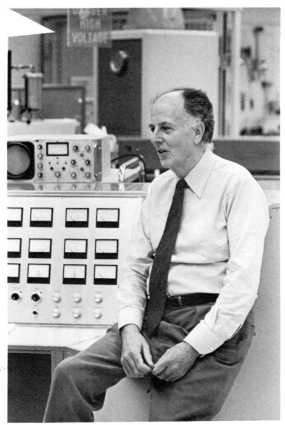

II

under the action
of absinth

to W. Mann.

Saturday

IV

This, my dear ~~Julian~~ Wilfrid, is
Bertie Russell, dreaming
(a I fear not adversely) of the
future. What a thing it is
(as Lapsley men said) to have
a Past. He is also reading
William of Ockham. Guy.

1/5 000 000

(16899) 25796/1301
2,050,000 8/40 JC&SLmt
Cp644/229
(REGIMENT)
CODE 5-34-0

Guy Burgess
1951

OVER

V

evening of his last day in Washington, 3 June , in spite of an exhausting round of visits, he gave up the opportunity of a few hours of well-deserved rest to come out to our house to dine with the civilian successor in charge of the nuclear-energy group at CIA.

A month later, on 8 July 1949, I drove the family up to Deep River so that they could spend the summer there in a house rented by us by friends and almost next door to our old home. I was able to spend a few days in the laboratories, my old haunts, before returning alone to my desk in Washington. I went north again in late August to collect Miriam and the children. Then within a few days of our return to Washington there occurred another landmark in nuclear history. Although the world was not to know about it until some three weeks later, the Russians had succeeded in detonating their first nuclear device, long before we had expected.*

The date was around 14 September. The time was 11.30 pm. I had one foot in the bath-tub when the telephone rang. It was Alex Longair, assistant science attaché at the British Embassy, to tell me that I had been invited to attend a session at a "war room" which was then situated not far from the White House, but which now no longer exists. I dressed and drove straight down town, arriving at my destination at about 1 am. Here I found an impressive gathering of service people scurrying hither and thither marking data on charts, and there were also several scientists with whom I was acquainted. I particulary remember a striking seven-foot globe whose twin had been placed in the White House for the use of the President. In a hurried briefing I learned that a radioactive cloud had been detected and then followed by the U.S. Air Force from the Pacific, across America and to the eastern shores of the Atlantic. At 3 am we adjourned to the Pentagon and held a top-secret teletype discussion with colleagues, including Michael Perrin (Deputy Controller-General of Atomic Energy, Ministry of Supply), gathered at the American Embassy in London. This discussion took the form of sequential teletype messages that appeared before us on two television screens, the one for outgoing and the other for incoming messages. I returned home at about 6 or 7 o'clock in the morning for a few hours' rest.

*As President Truman wrote: "I was surprised, of course, that the Russians had made progress at a more rapid rate than was anticipated" (*Memoirs*, vol II, p‡, Doubleday and Company Inc, Garden City, NY 1956).

Returning later in the day to the War Room I found it as busy as ever, with Major-General M R (Nellie) Nelson of the U.S. Air Force in charge of operations. As the sole British representative I must have been outnumbered by about fifty to one, and I recalled the "Admiral's" advice to call on Lord Tedder if in need. I therefore telephoned him at the Embassy and he immediately agreed to come and support me, but said he had no car. I told him I would be right along to pick him up. When we returned there was only a small parking space available outside the building in which the War Room was located, and it took two or three backward and forward passes before I could get into it, each time *gently* bumping the car behind or the one in front. Every time that I contacted one or other of these cars Lord Tedder would help me along by exclaiming "bumps-a-daisy"! When I re-entered the War Room, however, with a Marshal of the Royal Air Force in uniform the effect was magnificent. He was briefed by the major-general and his staff, and by the time he finally left my own position on the totem pole was significantly higher.

The "Admiral" and Bill Penney arrived from London at the invitation of the U.S. groups some time during the week-end of 17–18 September and stayed with us in our house. Bill had with him the results of radioactive analyses of the fall-out samples collected by the Royal Air Force from over the Eastern Atlantic. I played some small part in the report he wrote about it; but in the process of typing it became so highly classified that neither of us was allowed to proof read it.

On Tuesday or Wednesday I realized that the cloud of radioactive debris was straddling the 49th parallel and, as Canada was one of the "tripartite" countries, I asked one of the U.S. military staff if the Canadians had been informed. "No", I was told "we have informed you and the Canadians belong to you, don't they?" I explained that Canada was an independent country with its own Ambassador in Washington, and suggested that perhaps he could be informed. He was!

On 23 September 1949 President Truman announced that there was evidence that in recent weeks an atomic explosion had occurred in the U.S.S.R. A few days before that I had been allowed to cable through Peter Dwyer's channel to the Chief MI6 asking that the Prime Minister, Mr C R Atlee, be informed that there was *conclusive* evidence that the Russians had successfully detonated a nuclear device. For nine days I had been one of a relatively small group of people in the world outside Russia to know that "Russias had the bomb"; this was a very sobering thought, and it somehow made me feel that my shoulders were helping to carry the weight of the world.

Bill Penney returned home soon after the President's announcement but the strain had been too great for the "Admiral". He suffered a heart attack on 24 September and was taken to Garfield Memorial Hospital. The attack was not too severe however and we hopefully booked passage home for him on the *Caronia* on 11 October; the decision whether or not he could go depended on what the electrocardiograph showed on 8 October. This was, however, unsatisfactory and I asked the U.S. Air Force if they could possibly fly him back in an ambulance plane. I pointed out that he had come at their invitation although he was not in good health, having had a similar mild attack in January, and that it was important that we should get him home; and after some initial reluctance they agreed to do so.

At the beginning of November I received one of his cheery letters written from his home on 28 October. It begins with the salutation "To the Keeper of the Keys, from the Picker of the Locks — Greetings!" The first paragraph reads: "With reference to our 927 in answer to your 101, through a most indelicate source I think I have identified the person in question. The enclosed newspaper cutting refers". The cutting, which appears to be from one of the London evening newspapers, reads as follows:

MYSTERY NAVY MAN FLIES HOME ON A STRETCHER

A Royal Navy lieutenant-commander was flown on a stretcher from New York to London Airport to-day in a special Constellation of the U.S. Military Air Transport Services.

A doctor and a United States naval ambulance had waited all morning to meet the airplane.

The Commander was carried straight into the ambulance and driven away.

To all questions officials replied that the Commander's name could not under any circumstances be disclosed and that he came under the category of "top secret."

Neither would officials say what his injuries are.

Once we had adjusted ourselves to the new situation, we turned our joint efforts to the assessment of the Russian production capabilities. One swallow does not make a summer; nor did the detonation of one nuclear device imply the existence of a nuclear force.

A major change in our own organisation occurred in that Autumn of 1949 when Kim Philby arrived in early October to succeed Peter Dwyer as the MI6 representative in Washington — a replacement more momentous in the light of history than it seemed at the time. They overlapped for a brief period in the aftermath of the Russian atom bomb so that Philby was able to put himself fully in the picture of what had happened in the previous three weeks. After more than thirty years it is impossible for me to remember details but I am almost certain that he called on his sick colleague the "Admiral" in Garfield Memorial Hospital.

The winter passed uneventfully but in the spring of 1950 Sybil married a colonel in U.S. intelligence. As intelligence officers and secretaries are not permitted to marry other nationals both Sybil and her colonel had to resign from their respective intelligence assignments and Victoria was sent out by MI6 as a replacement. I had the pleasure and privilege of driving Sybil to her wedding, a context in which neither of my daughters has seen fit to trust my motoring skills. Victoria proved to be as highly efficient as Sybil in the arts of typing and the use of one-time pads. It is now possible to look back without too much irritation to the fact that my top-secret messages to London were put into one-time pad by Victoria and sent by commercial cable, whereas those with a higher classification were sent by Philby via "C". But my immediate reaction when I learned later of his defection was to feel that all the work I did during the eighteen months that we were together in Washington had been an almost complete waste of time.

During this latter period of my stay in Washington we became very friendly with Professor George Gamow and his wife Rho, and I attended one semester of his course of lectures on nuclear physics at George Washington University which helped me to keep in touch with my fast-fading profession.

My contract with the Ministry was due to end on 1 October 1950. Late in the preceding May I received a long letter from the "Admiral" about my future plans. The first decision that faced me was whether I wished to come back to England for good. If I did, I should then have to choose either to return to academic life or to stay on in the Ministry. He himself would much like to have me working with him over the next few years, but any such arrangement would be unlikely to carry what the Americans call tenure. While he did not want to influence me overmuch, he thought I ought seriously to consider whether I might not find better opportunities, for myself and for my family, if I stayed in North America instead of returning to a post-war Britain. If I did decide to stay, it might suit each of us if I extended my existing contract by another year, with a three-month termination clause on my side; this would give me plenty of time to look round.

It was a difficult and important decision to make. I was now over forty; and I had never been "established" in the Civil Service. For the moment I wanted to keep all options open. So in replying to the "Admiral" I said how much I appreciated his "thoughtful, considerate and kind" suggestions, and especially his generous offer of a further year in Washington. As he had made it clear when I joined him that he did not want anyone to stay in the job for more than two years, I looked on this extension as a great compliment. I therefore indicated that I should like to stay in Washington long enough to restore full co-operation with the nuclear-energy group at CIA, and that I should like to extend my tour of duty until the spring of 1951, when the family would be likely to find better weather on their return to England; at the same time I should appreciate it if he would enquire about any other possible openings at the Ministry.

About this time life that had become somewhat routine and humdrum in Washington was enlivened by the arrival of a defector. Strangely, I can remember his cover name but not his actual name; I could also pretty well pin-point the house where he was lodged and interrogated. An officer of MI6 was sent to Washington to join in the interrogation. One night stands clearly focused in my memory. We had asked the American side to see their assessment report and eventually, but reluctantly, they said we could have it for one night only. We spent that time gleaning what we could from it. I remember Victoria returning from a party at about 11 pm in evening dress, and she and I left the office together at about 6 am.

In June of the same year (1950) I had another pleasant and

unexpected interlude. Christopher Clarkson, the Civil Air Attaché, and Maurice Brown, Assistant Civil Air Attaché, were flying the Embassy de Havilland Dove west to attend a meeting of the Institute of Aeronautical Sciences in Los Angeles and they invited me to go with them so that I could visit my old friends and the new Radiation Laboratory at Berkeley. Christopher's wife, Maria Mannes, completed the party — or perhaps I should say that I completed it! While Christopher and Maurice piloted, Maria and I engaged in lively conversation in the small but very comfortable passenger compartment.

The trip was mainly uneventful. I found an Indian silver belt for Miriam in Albuquerque, we went through the San Bernardino Pass in a thunderstorm that gave me one of my most spectacular colour photographs, and we had to veer off suddenly to port while landing in Los Angeles because a small plane nipped in ahead of us. I flew up to San Francisco for a very happy reunion in Berkeley and then Christopher picked me up in San Francisco for the flight home.

It was in the same month that we held our one and only cocktail party, for about one hundred guests, on the occasion of a visit by Michael Perrin. The guest list was quite impressive, and included among others, in many cases with their wives, the Atomic Energy Commissioners and Carroll Wilson, the General Manager; Robert Le Baron, Deputy to the Secretary of Defense for Atomic Energy; Admiral R H Hillenkoeter, General M R Nelson (USAF), General K D Nichols (AEC) and Dr H D Smyth; Dr C J Mackenzie, President of the National Research Council of Canada, and Brigadier L H Nicholson of the Royal Canadian Mounted Police; Sir Frederick Hoyer Millar, Minister at the British Embassy and Lord Tedder. And after eighteen months on the job we felt that we had achieved some degree of Tripartite *rapport* in our own small field of interest.

During his visit I also told Perrin that, tentatively, I would like to accept a job he had offered me in the Technical Policy Group of the Directorate of Atomic Energy. In August 1950 I spent just under two weeks in England for discussions, going and coming on my two old favourites the *Queen Mary* and *Queen Elizabeth*, in very different shape, apart from a few surviving cockroaches, from their stripped-down wartime condition.

After this lapse of time, I cannot remember when we first met

Jim Angleton, then one of several CIA liaison officers, and his family. But it must have been in the autumn of 1950, and was probably after our eleventh change of address in as many years, when we moved to the pleasant incorporated town of Somerset just north of the DC-Maryland boundary off Wisconsin Avenue. We have many photographs of his orchids taken on the front porch of our old frame house in Somerset, and our sons Jaime and Peter became good friends for the short time remaining of our tour of duty. At the end of November the Angletons invited the Philbys and us to Thanksgiving dinner. That Thanksgiving we had two dinners, the first in the early afternoon with Walter and Martha Colby. At the Angletons the dinner was a lively occasion, with the Angletons and ourselves each contributing two children, and the Philbys most if not all of theirs, including Harry who was not more than a few weeks old.

In our remaining months we saw a fair amount of the Angletons and we recall many pleasant week-end visits to their home in the course of which we would also spend time in Jim's greenhouses admiring his magnificent orchids.

One of the perquisites at the Embassy was for a different member of the senior staff to take the bag to Cuba once a month. The bag went fortnightly but a King's Messenger was only available once a month, so we alternated with him. On 13 December 1950 this duty eventually fell to my lot. On the outward flight I sat on what in one sense was no longer a "top" secret bag, which I handed over to two security guards from the Embassy at the Havana Airport. I spent the next day sightseeing in Havana. Miriam had asked me to bring back some guava jelly and in the course of looking for it I was accosted at almost every street corner by someone soliciting for the "house of the twenty senoritas". That evening I was recommended to dine at the "Montmartre' but on my way to it from the Embassy a man sidled up to me and again asked if I wished to go to the house of the twenty senoritas. I declined, saying that all I needed at that moment was a drink. He responded by offering to take me to "the perfect place for a drink", and partly from thirst and partly from curiosity I yielded to his importunities. Even to my untutored eye it was very soon clear that the house into which he had taken me was something more than a drinking place — possibly even the house of the twenty senoritas, of whom there were several. There was a bar and I offered drinks to my guide and to one of the senoritas who had attached herself to us. They both chose "rum and cokes" which I did also — feeling that conformity was the better part of valour. Indeed, at this my aim was to make good my escape. When, therefore, the lady invited me to stay the night, or to remember her name if I should return, I pleaded a dinner date and left with my guide — but not before another lady in a green dress who seemed to be in charge insisted on showing me, with some pride, the green bedroom. Everything therein was green — and could be mine for seven and a half dollars. I told her I already had a satisfactory hotel room and as we reached the sanctuary of the sidewalk there flashed through my mind a new version of an English proverb, "Too many cokes spoil the brothel." Although I never returned I have to admit that I can still remember the name of the senorita.

The following day I flew back to Washington — this time with an enormous bag loaded with cigars for my less fortunate colleagues (and, I am pretty sure, with the guava jelly for Miriam). The only other event of any importance (and that has been vastly exaggerated) that happened before we left for England was the Philbys' dinner party which is described in the next chapter.

In the meantime, the "Admiral" had written to me on 24 January 1951, bringing me up to date about recent discussions in London aimed at correlating U.K. — U.S. intelligence estimates, and telling me that my successor was leaving on 23 February; he would however extend my period of service to "give quite a long overlap". He also warned me that Lord Portal, Controller General of the Directorate of Atomic Energy, Ministry of Supply, was definitely resigning on 1 August and that when Perrin, the Deputy Controller General for Technical Policy, left in May or June much of "his policy work will naturally gravitate to the office of the Under Secretary for Atomic Energy, namely How", leaving only the co-ordination between the various technical departments of atomic energy that might fall in my bailiwick.

The "Admiral" followed up this information with a further letter, written on 5 February 1951 and prompted by a report from Sam Goudsmit, who headed the post-war "Alsos Mission" that I might be offered an academic post in Ann Arbor. He urged me to think very seriously, both for the sake of myself and of my family, before I turned down such an opportunity, and he repeated, in rather stronger terms, the advice he had given me nine months earlier (see pp 70, 71 above) that I should consider the advantages of staying in the U.S.A. — a country where he knew I found myself very much at home — as against returning to an England that had changed so much since I had last worked there.

Reading his letters again so many years later, I am convinced that he was genuinely interested in our well-being. He had expressed himself most appreciatively, on two occasions, for what I had done: in Washington, at the time of the detonation of a Soviet nuclear device, he told me that he could not have had a better representative, while on my return to London he said that I had done the best job in the history of the liaison office. But perhaps the latter was not so very outstanding as the history of that office could not have covered a period of much more than ten years.

With regard to the imminent reorganization of the Directorate, the "Admiral" doubted if atomic-energy intelligence would remain in the Ministry of Supply, and he wrote: "However much I would like you to stay on with me over the next few years, the only assured future in the intelligence field lies in the SIS, and I am afraid there is not much chance of a man of your age being accepted as a career officer there."

I was, and remain, deeply grateful for his concern. In retrospect it may have been foolish of me to disregard his advice. But there were other more personal considerations to be taken into account. I wanted to help my mother with her affairs and also to dispose of the family business that had been more or less without leadership since my father's death.

I was influenced too by the arrival of a long-awaited letter from Michael Perrin. Writing on 13 February he told me much that I had already heard from the "Admiral", and added his own view that the coming changes "strengthened the argument that the whole of the Directorate of Atomic Energy would gain great benefit by having me in the Technical Policy Branch. Although the question of his successor had not been officially settled, I had reason to expect that I should inherit some part of the action. He warned me that I would have to revert, at least temporarily, to a lower grading, as the Establishment Branch held that the higher grade to which I had been promoted in November 1949 (with retrospective effect to my arrival in Washington nearly a year earlier) was tied to the appointment, but in his view (which he repeated in a later letter of 21 March) the question of my re-appointment to a higher grade of Senior Professional Scientific Officer could be considered fairly soon after my return. He summed up his first letter with the words: "A good case can be made for your return to Shell Mex House as soon as possible in order to get the maximum overlap here before I leave it if, as I sincerely hope will be the case, you now make up your mind definitely and accept the offer of this post in D. At. En. (T.P.)."

This letter encouraged me in the belief that there would at any rate be a worth-while job for me when Perrin left; and combined with the personal factors I have mentioned above it led us to decide that we would return to England as we had planned.

My successor and his wife arrived at the end of February and there began a round of cocktail parties and dinners to welcome them. I myself gave a farewell lunch at the old Cosmos Club to introduce him to about a dozen colleagues. We seem to have mislaid the list of guests but they included the highly respected and recently appointed Director of Central Intelligence, General Bedell Smith.

After about a fortnight, when it became known that we were not leaving until mid-April, the pace of the parties slackened; but in our last three weeks it became so intense that even then we felt we could never again face such an ordeal, however well meant. Nowadays, thirty years on, we certainly could not do so! We were invited out to dinner every single night in those three weeks. On top of this we had invitations to drinks before dinner, to lunch, and in the last week even to breakfast. American hospitality to friends knows no bounds, and when that was added to the hospitality of our friends from the British community, it is small wonder that we found it overwhelming.

At last, on 18 April 1951, we drove up to New York and boarded the *Britannic*. As soon as we had made sure the children were all right both Miriam and I collapsed on our beds and slept. Ostensibly we were returning to England for good. But the conflict between the advice we had received from the "Admiral" and from Perrin must have left a lingering uncertainty in my mind. I remember that in the matter of cars I hedged my bets. We took our Canadian car, an old friend from Chalk River days, with us on the *Britannic*; but we left a small Studebaker convertible for the time being in the garage of our good friends Kenneth and Jenny Thomson, the Colonial attaché at the British Embassy, and his wife, just in case we came back.

6
Washington — A Digression

I have already said something of my acquaintance with Bruno Pontecorvo (see pp 58–60 above) and of the good impression he made on my colleagues as well as on me while we were working together in Canada. Indeed it was because of the reputation he established at Chalk River that he was invited to accept a senior position at Harwell when the United Kingdom set up its own Atomic Energy Research Establishment. As Alan Moorehead wrote in 1952: "At no point had security any complaint about him. He was known as a man who never talked politics, not even atomic politics, and his associations were all with men of established loyalty in scientific work in North America."*

But the shock experienced by the western world at the arrests of Nunn May and Fuchs and the defection of Pontecorvo was as nothing to the outrage that was caused by the revelation of the double lives of Burgess and Maclean and, though not until 1963, of Kim Philby. They attracted more attention partly because the drama was so long-drawn-out, partly because, unlike their predecessors, they were "establishment" figures in a double sense. Each of them was a cradle member of the socio-political "establishment", and they all held offices of tenure under the Crown.

Each of them in his time was stationed in Washington. Maclean was

*Alan Moorehead, *The Traitors*, p 181, Hamish Hamilton, 1952.

appointed as First Secretary at the Embassy in May 1944, and as acting Head of Chancery a year later, and in 1947 he was nominated to serve as joint secretary of the Western Allies' Combined Policy Committee on atomic-energy development. He left the States in September 1948 for home leave before taking up a new post in Cairo. In an earlier chapter I have explained that whatever contacts he may have had with a mythical "Basil" it was quite impossible, on the facts, that I, Wilfrid Mann, could have been "closely involved" with him.

But during my stint of two and a half years in Washington, from 1948 to 1951, I did work under the same roof for some part of the time with both Burgess and Philby. With Philby, who arrived in the Autumn of 1949 to take over as MI6 liaison officer, I overlapped for some eighteen months; with Burgess, who did not arrive at the Embassy until a year later, for a very much shorter time. In view, however, of all the allegations that have been bandied about, I think it is worthwhile to assemble in this short chapter a brief but, to the best of my knowledge, complete account of my relationship with each of them.

Burgess, Philby and I, as well as Geoffrey Paterson, worked in the small main Chancery (and not its annexe), and our offices were all within an approximate 60-foot length of corridor. The Embassy was a very large organization but each of us had his own job to do and very little time or inclination to interact with others. This applied equally to my relationship with Burgess and Philby, especially as the latter maintained the strong cloak of secrecy that was appropriate to his position. Much of my own time I spent *outside* the Embassy, visiting the Departments of Defense and State, the AEC and the CIA. Miriam and I led an intense social life — lunches for me, cocktail parties and dinners for us both — but it was orientated mainly towards my American colleagues. (Occasionally Kris and Peter would smite our consciences by thinking it worthy of comment that we were actually spending an evening at home!)

Nor, as far as Burgess was concerned, did we find him personally attractive — and that is an understatement. His slovenliness, his bad manners, his drinking habits, his sheer effrontery, have been described often enough. It happened, however, that when he took up his appointment at the Embassy he was given an office diagonally across the corridor from me in the now demolished fourth side of the quadrangle overlooking Massachusetts Avenue. Our office looked out on the Avenue and his into the quadrangle. Our door, because we had files of deciphered intercepts, had an iron gate with a lock whose combination was only known to someone in Sir Robert Mackenzie's security office, and to Sybil, Victoria and me. My general impression of Guy was of a pretty uncouth character who sported a battered duffle coat, and who was always more or less the worse for wear owing to the combined effects of alcohol and diabetes. He was, however, invariably at his work, which seemed to be largely concerned with extracting articles from newspapers, before I arrived. As the door of his office was slightly nearer to the front entrance he would also almost always call out good morning and button-hole me for five or ten minutes before I could move along to my own office. He always had plenty to talk about. One morning it was to show me a cartoon that he had drawn of Ernest Bevin waiting on the cliffs of Dover with Hector McNeil, the Minister of State to the Foreign Office, waving to him from a motor-torpedo boat that was approaching the shore. There was a story to the cartoon. Guy was at that time a private secretary to Hector McNeil, whom the Secretary of State had summoned back from France for some urgent meeting of the Cabinet. The only means of returning rapidly was apparently by MTB (why not by plane is unknown to me but irrelevant) and Guy had drawn the cartoon which was then taken by McNeil to the Cabinet meeting. *Ipso facto*, and again I know not why, the cartoon had been entered as a Cabinet paper, classified Top Secret, and later given back to Guy. He now derived great amusement by leaving this "Top-Secret" paper on top of the contents of the unlocked middle drawer of his desk to see if the Embassy security staff would find it!

Later he gave me one of his caricatures, of Bertrand Russell contemplating the mushroom cloud from an atom bomb (Plate IV). This was initially inscribed to "Julian", whoever he may have been, and then re-inscribed to me.

Somewhat later still we held a dinner party in our Somerset residence to which we had invited Kim Philby's secretary and also the secretary of Dr Carroll Wilson the first General Manager of the Atomic Energy Commission. Guy Burgess gate-crashed the party on the excuse of bringing Kim's secretary. It was the only time he entered our house but while he was there he got hold of a book by George Gamow entitled

Atomic Energy (a subject on which he occasionally tried to sound me out!) and drew a caricature of one of the guests on the inside of the cover, and a psychologically interesting one of Stalin *eating* a marble table of the type one might find in a side-walk café in France. On the table is a bottle of Pernod (Plate IV). (Later we were to be present when he caricatured a lady at a dinner party that was to provoke many international repercussions.) Burgess was also a consummate name-dropper. He was "a friend of Hector McNeil" and when Anthony Eden spent a day in Washington in late 1950 it was Guy who was asked to tear himself away from his clipping of newspapers to show Eden around. With considerable satisfaction he showed me the bottle of Kentucky Gentleman that he claimed was a present from Eden — "Anthony Eden's favourite bourbon" he told me! Because of this story that has been previously recounted by others I hope that no future author will assign Anthony Eden a place in the hierarchical order of moles or "numbered" men, on the basis of guilt by association.

I shall refer shortly to the notorious dinner-party in which he played a leading role. My last memory of him is of an incident which occurred shortly before our departure. He caught me as usual one morning as I was passing his office door, and said he wanted me to do him a favour. He would appreciate introductions to our more intellectual American friends, because when the Philbys left at the end of their two-year term in Washington in the autumn of 1951 he would be left without the support of the parents and the company of the children. I was completely non-committal because I knew that Guy did not believe that such a phenomenon as an intellectual American existed. When I got home that night I told Miriam of his request and she almost exploded with: "Not on your life; not only would he ruin things with our friends but for your successor too!" With such an identity of feeling I never touched on the subject with Burgess again, nor did he raise it.

Kim Philby's was a very different character. Whatever his private life may have been, in public he was always suave, self-possessed, gracious, charming and erudite. Only later did we realize what powers of instant dissimulation he possessed. I remember that as Christmas 1950 approached we glanced, as we usually did, through the pile of cards we had received the previous year, to make sure that we did not, at any rate unintentionally, miss anyone out. Among these cards there happened to be one from Bruno and Marianne Pontecorvo, which they had sent to us in 1949 when they were still at Harwell. As a joke I took it into Philby's office, and put it on his desk in front of him saying "Look what we've got." The reaction was immediate. He leapt to his feet exclaiming, loudly and excitedly, "Where did you get this?" I said "From Harwell last year" and he sank back into his chair.

He had also some sense of humour. I remember that he liked to tell one story about Aileen going to their doctor because of a general feeling of malaise. The doctor's speciality happened to be diseases of the sinus, and he prescribed for her some form of radiant heat to be applied to the face. It soon turned out, however, that there was nothing the matter with her but another pregnancy. In fact both Miriam and I felt that Aileen was a lovely, long-suffering wife, who had somehow to cope with a hectic and chaotic social life, a large family, and a domestically helpless, often drunken, husband. But it was not until we read the description of him written by his third wife, Eleanor, that we realized quite how much any woman who married Kim Philby had to put up with.*

My main official contact with Philby lay in the fact that his office, which was just round the corner formed by Burgess's office, provided my channel for communicating to London information of the highest classification, a facility of which I had to make frequent use. But it would usually be Sybil (or later her successor Victoria) who took the message round to Philby's secretary to handle. Otherwise our paths did not cross much, either professionally or socially. Occasionally we met at a party or dinner, but certainly not more than once at the same house. I have mentioned that we ate Thanksgiving Day dinner in 1950 with the Philbys at the Angletons. We also gave two of the Philby children and their "nice Scottish nanny" (that was Miriam's description of her) a ride home, together with Kris and Peter, from the 1949 Christmas party for children given by Sir Oliver and Lady Franks at the Embassy. The Philbys had their American clientèle and we had ours.

It remains merely to give as accurate a record as I can of that dinner party given by the Philbys in January 1951 to which brief reference has

*Eleanor Philby, *Kim Philby: The Spy I Married* (Ballantine Books, New York, 1968) first published as *Kim Philby: The Spy I Loved*, by Eleanor Philby/Patrick Seale (Simon & Schuster Inc. New York, 1967).

already been made. I do so not because of its intrinsic importance but because it has already been described so often in print that it is already passing into folk-lore; and as so often with folk-tales, the various accounts of it which I have read differ in detail and indeed in some cases are inconsistent. Kim Philby himself, in his account, even gives a different name for the guests of honour. It is difficult to believe that he did so merely out of consideration for their feelings. I have a more personal interest too in that, according to the hypothesis put forward in *The Sunday Times* of 15 June 1980, (see p 119 below), my attendance at the dinner was used by Andrew Boyle as a means of indirectly connecting me with the "Fifth Man".

The sources used by the various authors are also interesting. One of them asked me for a personal interview and came to dinner as we had no other free time. I thought the information given was for background use only, and I was surprised when a distorted version of it was published without my permission. But perhaps this was a valuable lesson for me.

In all, then, there were about a dozen guests, many of whom have now been named. Human nature being what it is, it is only natural that what happened should get around an ever-widening circle. But I emphasize again that it acquired sinister overtones only in the light of after-events.

It began, as would any normal dinner, with *apéritifs*. It proceeded pleasantly and without any untoward incident and after dessert we adjoined to the living-room for coffee. It was at that point that Burgess entered. Neither Miriam nor I can recall that he came in "lurching"* and "obviously intoxicated",† nor that he approached the wife of the guest of honour "with raised arms"†. Nor was it "very late"† so the "customary nocturnal prowling"* must have been of rather short duration that evening because coffee was just about to be served; the time was probably not later than 9.30 pm.

Guy was however in his usual aggressive mood and, almost immediately after being introduced, he commented to the wife of the guest of honour that it was strange to see the face he had been doodling

---

The Climate of Treason: Five Who Spied for Russia, by Andrew (Boyle, Hutchinson of London) pp 360 & 361.
†*Philby: The Long Road to Moscow*, by Patrick Seale and Maureen McConville, (Hamish Hamilton, London, 1973), p 210.

all his life suddenly appear before him. She immediately responded by asking him to draw her. She was a pleasant woman but her jaw was a little prominent; Guy caricatured her face (and contrary to the account given by David Martin* he *only* drew her head as he had drawn the lady on the left of Plate V) so that it looked like the prow of a dreadnaught with its underwater battering ram. She immediately rose, took her husband by the arm, saying "I've never been so insulted in all my life, take me home", and they immediately left. Neither did we see the husband "swing" at Guy. Contrary to some other reports, this was really the end of an unpleasant incident. After a few minutes' embarrassment everything became very calm and I recollect sitting for twenty or thirty minutes with a friend on the low wall between the front garden and the sidewalk on Nebraska Avenue enjoying the cool of the evening while our wives conversed with the remaining guests inside. When we returned Kim Philby was in his shirt-sleeves, in bright red braces, and in tears on a small settee in what we recall as a smaller sitting room on the other side of the entrance hall, and Aileen had disappeared. The details are somewhat hazy — after thirty years, but both Miriam and I clearly remember seeing him in this state of extreme dejection.

The next act, so to speak, was when Guy took me into the kitchen and poured nearly half a tumbler of scotch into two glasses on the kitchen counter and proposed some health or other. No other guests joined us in this kitchen *tête-à-tête*; they were in fact beginning to depart. So after about three such mutual toasts I wandered back into the living room to find that Miriam had left with many of the other guests including our friend, who had joined me on the wall outside, and his wife. Miriam and I would often drive in separate cars to nearby dinner engagements, especially if they happened to be somewhat "official", so that if the gathering continued much beyond 10.30 or 11 pm she could go home to relieve the baby-sitter and leave me to cover the discussion.

The ubiquitous Washington cocktail parties were useful sources of background information, especially when someone after a few drinks would become very confidential and perhaps make a few injudicious remarks about the organization. George Gamow had a Russian proverb which translated as "What a sober man has on his mind, a drunk one has

Wilderness of Mirrors, by David C. Martin (Harper & Row, New York, 1980), pp 47 & 48.

on his tongue." Guy Burgess himself did not have a very high alcohol threshold in this respect, probably because he was a diabetic. Conversely, my own threshold — at any rate in those days: — was pretty high. As a rule of thumb I could take up to six martinis on an empty stomach, rather more if they were combined with something to eat, and still feel confident that I was in control of my head and my tongue. To say then, as one author* has done, that I was "too drunk to drive myself home" is just untrue.

In fact, when the time came to depart I was still sober enough to realize that after the kitchen session with Guy it would be better not to drive my car. The ambassador, Sir Oliver Franks, had a reputation for being tough on traffic offences, an attitude with which I fully agreed when it came to the too often abused diplomatic privilege. So even if I had had a minor mishap I knew that I would be in trouble! (Just a few months later, Kim Philby himself used this well-known trait of the ambassador to trick him into sending Guy Burgess home in disgrace.) It fortunately turned out that two of the guests who had not departed were Philby's secretary and her escort for the evening. I asked them, and they kindly agreed to give me a ride. I must have got in soon after midnight and was not feeling too much the worse for wear when Miriam took me back for my car in the morning.

After Miriam had driven off in her own car, somewhere between nine and ten o'clock I dropped in to the Philbys, probably to see how Aileen, whom we liked very much, had survived the night. After we had exchanged a few words she said to me "The boys are upstairs in bed. Why don't you go up to see them?" The sound of voices led me to the right door. As I entered it, I can still see Philby and Burgess in the double bed that was facing me. They were propped up on pillows, wearing pyjamas; one, or even both of them, may have been wearing a dressing-gown as well. They were drinking champagne together, and asked me to have a glass too as a pick-me-up. I did not linger after drinking it because I had a series of engagements that morning. I had to call at CIA headquarters, then see two CIA colleagues off from National Airport, *en route* to visit the "Admiral" in London, to correlate our intelligence estimates, and then return to the Embassy. In the short time that I was

---

The Climate of Treason, Five Who Spied for Russia, op. cit.

with them, however, I got the impression that both Philby and Burgess were enjoying the situation immensely. I saw nothing more of either of them that day.

The situation made me feel puzzled and uncomfortable rather than alarmed. Aileen had treated the whole matter lightly and almost flippantly. I did *not* get the impression that the situation was homosexual in the sense that the two of them had spent the night together (indeed I gathered that one or both of them had already paid an early morning visit to the Embassy before my arrival). And I should emphasize that in that age of innocence thirty years ago neither I, nor most people of my generation, appreciated that a married man with a large family could also be a practising homosexual.

Certainly I had not enough to go upon to report a possible risk to security. After all, Philby was, on the surface at least, on terms of friendship both with Geoffrey Paterson, MI5's representative in Washington, and with Sir Robert Mackenzie, the Regional Security Officer. I should have felt it was distasteful and embarrassing to bring to their notice an incident which had no obvious security implications. Yet I could not help feeling uncomfortable and concerned by this epilogue to the party which only Aileen and I witnessed. Perhaps that is why I remember it so well.

When I returned to England and reported to the "Admiral" I did think it my duty to tell him about this particular incident, but even as I was talking I realized that he was not at all impressed. And why should he have been? In spite of our friendship and our mutual loyalty, I was still in one sense an outsider, and here I was expressing doubts about the strange behaviours of a senior officer of MI6, a colleague to whom the code of ethics of the day demanded the "Admiral's" complete loyalty. There was no more to be said.

To round off the story, it was not until early in 1952, when I was once more settled in the U.S.A. that I had the opportunity of telling Jim Angleton that I was still unhappy about the events of the morning after the Philbys' party a year ago. My concern had certainly not been lessened by the defection of Burgess and Maclean some months previously. He invited me to lunch at his home, together with one of his colleagues, and I recounted to them what had happened when I returned to the Philbys to pick up my car. Jim asked me if I would allow him to transmit this information to the British authorities, and I replied that of course I had no objection. I only hoped that now they would take it more seriously. It was a great relief to me to be able to unload my concern on someone who could share my feelings; but what happened afterwards I neither knew nor tried to find out, for I was by then working in a very different field.

7
England — An Interlude

To take up the story again from Chapter 5, we arrived back in England on 27 April 1951, and drove down to our old home in Belvedere Court in Putney, where my mother, after my father's death, had established residence in a flat on a lower floor. She was thus for a change able to enjoy the company of her grandchildren every day.

I duly reported for duty at the Directorate of Atomic Energy, in Shell Mex House, first to bring the "Admiral" up to date on his affairs in Washington and then to learn about my new job. The next few months were about the most depressing of my life. I found that my *only* regular assignment was to represent the Directorate of Atomic Energy at fortnightly meetings of the Cabinet Advisory Committee on Atomic Energy chaired by Sir Roger Makins. The only discussions of outstanding importance that I recollect at that time centred around the question of where the first British nuclear device should be tested. I visited all three main establishments (research, weapons and production) to establish lines of communication with them. In July Miriam and I had the pleasure of being asked to look after friends from Washington, AEC Commissioner Keith Glennan, Robert Le Baron who was now Chairman of the AEC Military Liaison Committee, and Mrs Le Baron, who were briefly in England on their way to meet Generals Eisenhower and Norstad in France. And for about three weeks in July we had a very pleasant vacation driving from Denmark (where we visited the Martensen-Larsen's and had lunch with Professor and Mrs Bohr in Tisvilde) south to Switzerland, with our Chalk River friends Ken and José Allen.

After Michael Perrin and then Lord Portal retired in the summer there was a complete hiatus at headquarters. It was generally expected that a Conservative government would be elected in November and that Lord Cherwell would again become the dominant scientific influence in government. In such a climate no one was prepared to make the slightest move in any direction.

I now began to realize that the "Admiral's" advice had been both wise and sound. I had been too long out of the country to fit back easily into the system, especially so because after all these years of government service I was still only a *temporary* civil servant, one who had been taken on to meet specific emergencies and at a higher salary or grade than I could have been given as an established officer. I was also to learn that, after his resignation, the written expectations of an official as senior as Michael Perrin had no clout whatsoever with an all-powerful "Establishment Division".

I had not yet however severed all my American links. Perhaps the car I had left with the Thomsons (p 76 above) was a symbolic hostage to fortune. It happened that while I was in Washington I had been asked, in late 1950 or early 1951, to give a seminar at the National Bureau of Standards (NBS) to describe my own pre-war research, and in March 1951 I had been offered a position as chief of the Radioactivity Section, which, of course, I had then declined. On 2 June when I had already realized the complete emptiness of my job in London, I wrote to the NBS Personnel Division to see if this position was still open. Lauriston S Taylor, Chief of the Atomic and Radiation Physics Division, wrote back on 7 June to affirm that it was open and offering it to me subject however to a loyalty clearance that might take several months. On 11 September he cabled me to say that my loyalty check had been completed and my appointment approved subject to receipt of a medical-examination form that had to be filled in in England.

The choice was a difficult one. For some weeks I hesitated before making what seemed likely to be a final break with the Old World. The moment of decision came in September, when I went to the

Establishment Division with Perrin's letter of 21 March in my hand (p 75 above), and was informed gently but bluntly that the *ex* Deputy Controller General's encouragement was not worth the paper on which it was written; that only the officers in Establishments could write such letters. I thanked them and told them that I would resign to accept a position in Washington; I submitted my resignation on 29 September to be effective from 1 November. Because of accrued annual leave I left the Ministry on 16 October, having received the usual notes from an Under Secretary and from an Assistant Secretary with thanks on behalf of the Minister "for all the good work you have done in the service of this Ministry". Cynically, perhaps, I thought that such gratitude, even expressed as kindly as it was and through the Establishment Division, might also be worth but little more than the paper on which it was written. My exchange of letters* with John Cockcroft gave me greater satisfaction.

As soon as I had resigned, I formally accepted the offer of appointment at NBS and began to make arrangements for my move back to America. I did not realize what interminable delays there were to be before the Department of State would approve my immigration visa, which I did not receive until 1 December.

In the meantime I was without work for nearly two months and by the middle of November (as I was not only unemployed but also unpaid) checked on my status at the Putney employment exchange. It appeared that I was in fact eligible to draw the dole but we felt that we should defer that drastic step for the time being as it might seem to be an unusual development for someone who had formerly been an attaché at the Embassy in Washington and alternate to the U.K. delegate to the United Nations Atomic Energy Commission in Lake Success.

The delay in receiving my visa was obviously due to my association with Pontecorvo and Burgess which I have recorded in some detail in previous chapters. These associations were of course no closer, no more intimate, than those of scores of my colleagues. It was only in the light of subsequent events that they had become of interest. This fact was confirmed to me in a very lively discussion with, by good fortune, a very

*Letter of October 1951 to Sir John Cockcroft from W B Mann, p 157 in Appendix A.
Letter of 23 October 1951, from Sir John Cockcroft to W B Mann, p 158 in Appendix A.

pleasant and competent vice-consul, Olive Jensen, at the American Consulate General in London. She had been fully informed by Washington of my associations with Bruno Pontecorvo and Guy Burgess and questioned me closely about them. I expressed strong doubts whether Pontecorvo ever was a spy, but I made it clear that I held no brief for Burgess. The question of Donald Maclean did not come up because I had never known him. In an article on 21 November 1979 in the *Washington Post* an old NBS colleague was quoted as saying that my security check had shown that I had known Maclean. It transpired, however, that he had never had access to my security file and, in a subsequent sworn statement he wrote that this allegation "must be considered as erroneous" and that it was elicited by a reporter's "persistent questions about MacLean (*sic*) and Dr Mann's association with him, Philby and Burgess .... His main point of interest seemed to be focused on MacLean and, quite frankly, I recall so little of the case that Philby, MacLean, and Burgess are synonymous in my mind."

I eventually left for New York on 5 December on the *Queen Elizabeth*. In the meantime Kris and Peter had both practically finished the autumn term at Roehampton School and we were loath to interrupt their education when they had progressed so far into the school year. Nor was it possible to move house at such short notice, so we decided that Miriam and the children would stay in London while I went to the U.S. I arrived in New York on 10 December and was welcomed in Washington by Kenneth and Jenny Thompson and reported next day for duty at the National Bureau of Standards. We had been embarrassed that our indecision had prevented our disposing of our car and that Kenneth and Jenny had been stuck with it so long. But if it were a nuisance they never admitted it, and it was naturally a great advantage for me to have it immediately available. I was made very much at home by the Thompsons, and I stayed with them for some three weeks, over Christmas, until I was able to rent a very pleasant room in Bethesda.

8

Washington —
A New Career

And so, for almost thirty years, I have worked with the National Bureau
of Standards at Washington, as Chief of its Radioactivity Section from
1951 until my retirement — already extended two years beyond the
previously normal age-limit — in 1980; and in semiretirement at NBS I
am still very fully occupied attending meetings and conferences on their
behalf on both sides of the Atlantic. To chronicle my scientific activities
over this period would not be of interest to the general reader. To record
the number of committees I have served, either as chairman or as
member, the number of international conferences I have attended,
would be even more tiresome.

I have also played a fairly active part in the communication of
scientific research and information. I was Editor of the *International
Journal of Applied Radiation and Isotopes* from 1965 to 1976, and I
remain Editor-in-Chief for North America. Since 1973 I have been
Editor of the *International Journal of Nuclear Medicine and Biology,* since
1977 Editor of *Environment International* and I still hold both
appointments. I have also done some part-time teaching as Adjunct
Professor in the Department of Chemistry at the American University in
Washington from 1961 to 1969. The second edition of a book I co-

authored with R L Ayres and S B Garfinkel, *Radioactivity and Its Measurement*, was published in 1980. Before leaving England in 1951 I received a London doctorate of science (DSc) degree, in 1958 I was awarded the U.S. Department of Commerce Gold Medal for Exceptional Service, and in 1977 I received the NBS Edward Bennett Rosa Award. In 1978, just before my expected mandatory retirement, I was elected President of the International Committee for Radionuclide Metrology.

My justification for this terse summary is that I do not want these recollections to lose a sense of perspective. In the two remaining chapters I deal with the occasions when the outside world disturbed the even tenor of a scientist's life. If I do so in some detail it is because I must if I am to achieve my aim of correcting the misstatements that have already been disseminated — some innocently, some deliberately — and of putting the record straight once and for all. But I regard the semi-political controversies into which I have been drawn as unsought interruptions, which must be seen against the background of a busy and varied professional career. My real life, for nearly one-third of a century, has centred round the National Bureau of Standards, and I like to think that in my own special field I have been of some service not only to NBS but also, through my external activities, to science generally.

But these incursions were in the future. My first decade with the NBS was uneventful and devoted to the pursuit of science. After six months' separation from my family I returned to England on the maiden voyage of the *United States* in July 1952. I came back in August in the same ship. Miriam and the children followed eight days later in the *Queen Mary*. Since then my work with international committees and conferences has necessitated my return to England and other countries in Europe at least once a year, occasionally two or three times. Until 1959 I attended such meetings more or less in a personal capacity, because as an alien I could not officially represent the National Bureau of Standards (although I was in fact doing so unofficially).

By the time however that I had been awarded the Gold Medal in 1958 I felt that it was time for me to accept the fact that my future career was in the service of the Bureau and that in order to act as its official representative abroad I should become an American citizen. I was naturalized in 1959, with my friends and colleagues Dr Lille Fano and

Dr Raymond W Hayward as sponsors. Citizenship was neither *given* to me in the 1940s nor forced on me then or later. By a strange circumstance I may even have dual citizenship because it was only later that the Supreme Court ruled that it was unconstitutional for a naturalized citizen to be deprived of his citizenship. Thus one was not required in 1959 to renounce one's citizenship of birth, in order to provide against the possibility of statelessness. I was warned at that time, however, that if I were to use my then still valid British passport I could be deprived of my U.S. citizenship.

About this time I was phoned one day by the British Broadcasting Corporation asking if they could interview me as one of the "brain drain". I replied that I could probably be better classified as the latter rather than the former, but they sent out a reporter and television equipment to my laboratory to interview me and I understand that it appeared on a programme entitled "Gallery 3". I explained that I looked upon myself more as an exile than a part of the brain drain. In retrospect I now feel that I could not have done nearly as much of what has been, I hope, productive work if I had stayed in the U.K. I had stayed out of the U.K. too long, as a useful, atomic-energy link between the U.K. and the U.S. and Canadian governments. With the assumption of my new job at NBS I would now have worked in or had access to nuclear research laboratories of all three member nations of the Tripartite Agreement, and many more.

A couple of personal memories remain from those early years. Sir Henry Tizard phoned us soon after we returned to Washington in 1952 and visited us for dinner, and we were able to arrange for Merle Tuve to join us and they reminisced about the war, radar and the Tizard Mission. He phoned again a few years later and gave us the great pleasure of coming again to dinner. It must in fact have been about 1957 because our younger daughter, Janet, was about two and he took her up in his arms and she plucked at his moustache and said "What's this?" At about this time Niels Bohr also came to Washington to receive the Ford "Atoms for Peace" award, and I visited him and Mrs Bohr at the home of the Danish ambassador. It was the last time that I was to see him and he spoke at length on his hopes, based on conversations with Churchill and Roosevelt, for openness in science after the war.

In 1956 we acquired a house in Chevy Chase, just over the District

Line in the State of Maryland. The younger members of the family are now scattered, but it remains our family home. After all these years I naturally regard myself as an American in every sense of the word; but apart from the international freemasonry of science I have retained many links with my native country. I was working in a rapidly expanding field of applications of radioactivity in which co-operation, based on the tripartite agreement reached at the Quebec Conference, was still very strong. Washington is in any case a very cosmopolitan place, Our close friends are scattered all over Europe and North America and far beyond. They include many "scientific" or "diplomatic" families who have sojourned in Washington either as visitors to our laboratory at NBS or as representatives at their countries' embassies. The scientific community especially is one that transcends most national frontiers.

My frequent visits to England, on personal or professional matters, have meant that I still feel at home there as I do also in Montreal, Ottawa or Deep River. I probably saw more of my mother in her last years (as she saw more of us and our children) than I might have done if we had been living in England. We had kept our flat in Putney for some years against the possibility of an eventual return. When we came back in 1958 to close it up, Miriam, Janet and I spent about a month there, with my mother occupying a flat downstairs in the same building. Apart from my sister's family, I have also kept closely in touch with my two cousins and their families (they come, unusually, from the same genetic pool as myself, for my father's brother married my mother's sister). Between them, they and their families muster four MDs and one SRN. I have mentioned that our son Peter spent two years in the sixth form of an English School. We still have a photograph of him being presented with other prefects to Princess Margaret on the occasion of her visit to the School; and he starred in a documentary film of school life, which in those days was more of an innovation than it would be now. During the shorter vacations he enlarged his experience of England; at least one Easter holiday he spent working in a brewery. Kris, our elder daughter, spent a year in 1959 at the Töchterschule in Zurich. Both of them graduated from McGill.

Personally, there is nothing I enjoy more than being on board a ship either in the northern reaches of the Atlantic or in that little appendage known as the Caribbean. I have been described as a "mid-Atlantic man". Perhaps in a former existence I was a citizen of that mythical lost island of Atlantis which is supposed to lie sunk in the ocean somewhere between England and America.

Such is the background against which the reader must set the drama — the melodrama? of the next two chapters. But, in conclusion, let me acknowledge that I would probably have not survived to write either them or the rest of this short book if it had not been for the dedicated care given to me by my old friend of 55 years, Cyril Barnes, into whose hospital at Hillingdon, Middlesex, I was providentially rushed following a serious haemorrhage after arriving in London Airport from Paris in November 1967. As a result of this unexpected and extended sojourn, over Christmas, in Hillingdon Hospital, I made one of my longest recent visits to England. Naturally, it enabled me to see much more of friends and family than did my usual transits of two or three days—and with a minimum of travelling because they came to see me!

9
Mr 'S' and Other Encounters

Apart from my scientific activities life passed fairly uneventfully until 1961 when, for two years, I apparently became of low-key interest to the KGB. In 1958 my NBS colleague, Dr Howard H Seliger, and I authored NBS Circular 594 entitled *Preparation, Maintenance, and Application of Standards of Radioactivity*. It happened that in January 1960 we were visited by Dr V V Bochkarev of Glavatom, Moscow, and he was given, among other things, a copy of this Circular.

In February 1961 I received a call from a Mr "S" of the Soviet Embassy in Washington, DC asking me to have lunch with him as he had "something of interest" for me. I met him for lunch and the "something of interest" turned out to be a letter from Dr Bochkarev together with two copies of a Russian version of NBS Circular 594, with a new preface written by Bochkarev, and replete with all the illustrations of the original, showing many of our colleagues of the NBS Radioactivity Section engaged in their various scientific pursuits. Mr "S" himself, as I learned later from him, was on assignment from the Soviet Scientific Research Institute of Medium Machinery, a category of machinery that included nuclear reactors. I also learned from "confidential sources" that "S" was an identified member of the Soviet

KGB. There followed, over a period of two years, a series of lunch-time meetings with "S" that took place at the Burgundy, Flagship, Piccolo, or Roma restaurants, and at the Cosmos Club. I kept in close touch with my "confidential sources", but my contacts were well content to leave me to handle the matter and decided it was not necessary to keep our meetings under surveillance. Actually the opportunity of doing this would have been limited as "S" would usually not telephone me until 10 or 11 am of the day that he wanted me to have lunch with him; we inadvertently discovered on one occasion that he was phoning from a drugstore. He also invariably walked several blocks from his car to our arranged meeting place, and would never permit me to accompany him back after lunch. At Christmas in 1962 he arrived unexpectedly at our house with a present of caviar and vodka, and we invited him in, but he said that Mme "S" was in the car. I said that I would like to go with him to wish her C HOBbIM ГОAOM but he replied that the car was too far away. It was an interesting and well-known technique but it must have involved a lot of walking in both clement and inclement weather.

"S" was a pleasant and an intelligent man and our lunch-time discussions were never dull. I have many pages of notes about them and they make interesting reading although they are nearly twenty years old. The conversation would usually proceed uneventfully until he reached the point where he thought it appropriate to raise the subject that was the reason for the invitation to lunch. And then he would almost invariably introduce it with the phrase "Oh, I forgot", or "Oh, I nearly forgot." On one such occasion, on 27 November 1961, we reached the point where he had "nearly forgotten" and he then delved into several of his pockets before producing a slip of paper on which was written the information that he would like to have. The information that he wanted was usually already available from published sources; on this occasion it referred to the allowable levels of radiation for personnel at atomic-industry establishments, the allowed levels of radioactive contamination of equipment and personnel, and the degree of pollution of "water basins, atmosphere, and territory in the neighborhood of atomic facilities". Any information that I gave him was cleared beforehand by my "confidential anonymous monitoring connections" and, on this particular occasion, he suggested that I should have lunch with him again "at his invitation" when I had collected the information. I replied that this would be very pleasant, but suggested that he should be my guest next time at the Cosmos Club. He seemed, however, to be perturbed at this invitation and said that I might not be "comfortable" giving him the information at the Cosmos Club; but I assured him that I would be quite comfortable; and probably thereby weakened my credibility! He nevertheless suggested that we meet at noon on Monday 11 December and said that he would phone me to arrange some other place for lunch than the Cosmos Club. On another occasion (28 January 1963) he told me that he could repay me for any expense that I might incur in obtaining reports (this time one on a Congressional inquiry on underground nuclear tests) as he had plenty of money for the purpose from the Academy of Sciences of the U.S.S.R.

Sometimes I would take him to lunch with one or two NBS colleagues in order to relieve the tension of our more prolonged and profound *tête-à-tête* and to avoid any semblance of receiving "gifts" contrary to federal fiat. But the "confidential anonymous keepers of my conscience" gave me an assured, but anonymous, absolution in this matter. When, however, "S" called me at 11.15 one morning to invite me to lunch at noon the same day and I asked him to have lunch with me and a colleague instead, he said that he wished to speak with me alone and would therefore like me to lunch with him.

The following brief summary of the highlights of my meetings with "S" may still be of some interest despite the passage of so many years:

(1) *Last week in February 1961.* "S" asked me to lunch to deliver letter from V V Bochkarev and two copies of Russian edition of NBS Circular 594.

(2) *3 March 1961.* Lunched with "S" and NBS colleague at the Cosmos Club and gave "S" my reply to V V Bochkarev.

(3) *26 October 1961.* "S" raised questions about Berlin and the recent testing by the Soviets of their first 50-megaton bomb. He asked me what I thought of the latter and I replied "Not much." He responded that the bomb was purely a defensive measure and I asked against whom — Eskimos, as they would receive much of the fall-out? I also suggested that "S" lay in a supply of canned milk to protect his small boy from getting too much strontium-90. "S" said, on parting, that the discussion had helped him!

(4) *27 November 1961.* Discussed disarmament and the inability of the

Soviets to accept inspection of nuclear testing because they considered such inspection would constitute, he said, espionage in the field of conventional armaments. He asked for the information mentioned above that related to nuclear industrial facilities. We briefly discussed the 22nd Congress.

(5) *21 December 1961.* Took "S" and NBS colleague to lunch at the Cosmos Club and gave him copies of NBS Handbooks 69 and 80 for Dr Bochkarev. Discussed Soviet and Chinese systems. "S" stated that where the former had one million qualified people from which to chose 10 politicians, the latter had only 100 from which to choose. "S" complained about our giving nuclear weapons to Germany. He also said I was a good diplomat as well as being a good scientist. I denied the latter part of the statement, but did not mean, by implication, to accept the former.

(6) *25 May 1962.* Received three more Russian translations of NBS Circular 594 with letter from Dr Bochkarev. We discussed the possibility of visiting Dr Bochkarev's laboratory where intercomparative measurements of our carbon-14 standards were to be made. By way of sounding out the background of "S" 's interest in me I wondered aloud if during such a visit I might see my old friend Bruno Pontecorvo again, and possibly Guy Burgess whom I had known. He made no comment about the former but said he had never met Burgess or heard of him. I said: "Never heard of him?" — "No." "Had he heard of Maclean?" — "No." and this last with an emphatic shake of his head. I found these replies interesting. "S" said that changes were taking place in the Soviet Union, but that the standard of living had to be improved, and the Internal Ministry and the "cruel police" eliminated.* In fact, the Internal Ministry would be eliminated in the near future, and policing would be taken over by local communities. By way of example, he said that it would be as if, every so often, my colleagues and I at NBS were to put on red armbands and patrol the neighbourhood. He said that hoodlums were disappearing from the streets of the Soviet Union. "S" also remarked upon the ingrained custom in this country of being "made to take" bread and water in a restaurant. I expressed the hope that the communists would never make such a terrible mistake.

---

*I later learned on 5 November (qv) that "S" did not appear to understand the meaning of the word "cruel".

(7) *3 October 1962.* "S" expects to be recalled around Christmas or in the Spring. His boy had been at summer camp but his wife had had no vacation. He was interested to know why we attached so much importance to underground nuclear tests. I suggested one or two reasons and he asked if any reports might be available; he realised that some might be classified. I told him that I knew of none, but if I heard of any being released I would keep him in mind. We had a fairly long discussion on the pro's and con's of a nuclear-test ban, which however he tended to confuse with the question of abolishing nuclear weapons. I pointed out that such a ban would be a small but welcome step in the direction of general disarmament. I said that I was in favour of a ban on all testing in the atmosphere or under water, but would permit underground tests of devices of less than 10- or 20-kiloton equivalence. He disagreed as this would permit the development of tactical weapons. He said that the Soviet Union had detected four (?) French underground nuclear tests in the Sahara Desert on 1 May by seismograph. He drew diagrams to illustrate the differences between records of earthquakes and underground nuclear events, the frequencies of recorded waves from the latter being about double those from the former. He thought that the sensitivities of the most sensitive Soviet seismographs were not greatly different from ours. He indicated that the U.S.S.R. might be willing to accept *ad hoc* inspection after our recording such an event, but would not accept general inspection.

(8) *5 November 1962.* "S" had ordered Martinis when I arrived and proposed my health and that of the international situation; it was because of this, he immediately informed me, that he wanted to see me. In particular, there had been an agreement between the U.S. and the U.S.S.R. on Cuba but Castro was refusing to observe it. What was going to happen? He thought that this might not be the last crisis because there were people in Russia who might want Kruschev to be firmer with the United States. He complained about the attitude of the American press and television. He was surprised at Kruschev's reaction as he had expected him to be more angry. I asked if Kruschev might be experiencing opposition in Russia and he said that of the 500 members of the Central Committee certainly not everyone saw eye-to-eye with Krushev. It was a long discussion. He said he was always interested in talking with me because I was so "cruel" to the politics of both systems.

On my expressing surprise at his use of the word "cruel" he said that perhaps he meant "persistent", from which I was led to suggest "hard" to which he agreed. I had earlier caused him to laugh heartily, which was quite unusual, when on asking me why we could not reach an agreement on nuclear testing I replied that it was probably because both sides were so bloody-minded! I gave him a letter for Dr Bochkarev.

(9) *13 November 1962.* To avoid indebtedness and to relieve the strain of our increasingly intense discussions, I had invited "S" to lunch with the two NBS colleagues with whom I lunched periodically. The conversation was relatively innocuous and pleasant, and dealt with Mikoyan, Cuba and the danger to world stability arising from "overcrowded" countries. He gave me two tickets for the Bolshoi Ballet that was then in Washington, DC.

(10) *28 January 1962.* "S" said that he had been ill in December and was returning to Moscow in the Spring. He mentioned that a Dr Petrasantz (?) was now in charge of Glavatom in succession to Professor V S Emalyanov. We spoke about South America where he said it was necessary to build up industry in order to disseminate wealth and to create middle classes, trades-union movements and a movement away from agrarian conditions. I inquired whether this was what Russia planned to do in Cuba and he said "Yes, to some extent." They hoped, for example, to mechanize the production of sugar. He also said that the British were building a fishing port in Cuba. I questioned this last statement and he reaffirmed that it was indeed the British who were helping the Cubans to build a fishing harbour! At this point he again introduced the topic of importance with "Oh, I forgot", and said that one of his friends had told him that there had been a report of a Congressional inquiry into underground explosions, issued about three weeks ago and he would be very pleased if I could get it for him. I told him that I had seen one about ten days or two weeks previously on the effects of nuclear weapons. He thought that this was not necessarily the one, but he would appreciate a copy of this one too. He would repay me for any expense, but I told him that I could probably get the reports for him without cost.* He referred again to the possibility of my being

*I later identified these two reports as "Destruction and Identification of Nuclear Explosions: Developments in the Field" and "The Effects of Nuclear Explosions" (a joint study by the Atomic Energy Commission and the Department of Defense).

invited to Russia to give some lectures, but wondered if I might need assistance in meeting the expense. I told him that, in the event, NBS might be able to support my travel, depending upon the state of the budget at that time. He added that if I were invited my expenses in Russia would be met by them and that I could also expect to receive some royalties from the translation of NBS Circular 594.

This was to be my last lunch with "S" as both he and his wife had been unwell. I doubt whether the two reports that he requested would have been cleared in time to give to him. He and his wife did, however, come to dinner with us at home on, I believe, Tuesday 9 April 1963, and we certainly discussed letters that I had addressed to the Editor of *The Washington Post* on the subject "Testing without Fallout" and which that journal had published on 6 and 16 April.*

I had quite enjoyed my interaction with "S" and I had wondered if I might be solicited by his successor, but I was not. Our exchanges had been frank but had never reached a point where he had asked me for any but published material, nor had I ever responded to his offers to repay me for expenses. I had also tried to return his hospitality and to avoid too great indebtedness to him. Probably, therefore, I did not conform to the "correct" pattern of behaviour. On the one occasion that I did try to sound him out on Burgess and Maclean I drew a completely blank response that I did not find to be credible. I felt that Burgess or Philby, the latter of whom was in Beirut during this period, might have given him a lead to me after he had first established contact on behalf of Bochkarev, but I never obtained any evidence of this, apart, possibly and negatively, from his strenuous and almost unbelievable denials of having ever heard of either Burgess or Maclean. This was especially puzzling as on one occasion he told me that while he had been reading the American press for four years he still avidly sought Russian news and would rather go hungry than to be deprived of it. He seemed to enjoy debate for its own sake, and he may have fostered our continuing association just because he wanted to proselytize a hopeless non-conformist. He was always a gentleman and never gave me serious cause for offense; possibly less than I gave him! Nearly twenty years later,

---

*Letters of 6 and 16 April 1963, from W B Mann to the Editor of *The Washington Post*, reproduced on p 159 in Appendix A.

especially as he was suffering from a heart ailment to which he may have long since succumbed, it would be discourteous to identify him more closely.

The next twelve years of our lives were politically peaceful and in my particular brand of science, the measurement of radioactivity and nuclear-decay data, relatively successful. I have said that I taught radiochemistry from 1961 until 1969 at the American University and I also acted as alternate to the Sectretary of Commerce on the Federal Radiation Council. During this time, however, two events took place that were to give rise to the wildest of rumours and eventually to equally wild scenarios involving me. The first was the alleged loss of a large amount of enriched uranium from a nuclear plant in Pennsylvania; the second was the diversion of about 200 tons of uranium ore or "yellow cake" belonging to Euratom which was being shipped by freighter from Antwerp to an Italian port. These two events had, however, one thing in common, namely that both the enriched uranium and the yellow cake were widely supposed to have been diverted to Israel.

These two events merely formed the backdrop for the main action. On 21 August 1975, two adjoining articles, one above the other, appeared on the front page of *The Times* of London. The one at the top of the page was titled "CIA 'gave technological support to Israel to make atomic bomb after 1956 Suez war'." The other "Dr Kissinger arrives in Israel today." The first article read as follows:

The Central Intelligence Agency (CIA) in 1957 and 1958 provided the Israelis with the technological support needed to help them manufacture the atomic bomb, it was disclosed yesterday.

According to Tad Szulc, former foreign and diplomatic correspondent of *The New York Times,* the operation was carried out by the CIA's Counterintelligence Staff, then headed by Mr James Angleton, the man dismissed last December when Mr William Colby, the director, and his agency came under fire for alleged illegal domestic activities.

Mr Szulc is now a freelance and has contributed to *Foreign Affairs Quarterly.*

Writing in the September issue of *Penthouse* magazine, he says: "Although the details of the Israeli nuclear enterprise are still top secret, it is known that, in the wake of the 1956 Suez War, the Eisenhower Administration resolved to provide Israel with all possible help in developing an atomic weapon. The Israelis had the theoretical knowledge, but they needed technological support at their Dimona nuclear research centre in the Negev Desert."

According to top intelligence sources, Mr Szulc says, "the CIA was charged with the responsibility of providing this support to the Israelis — and Angleton directed the effort.

Several nuclear scientists were secretly sent to Israel to work with Dimona scientists. The most important of them was a British born physicist, now an American citizen working for the United States Government in Washington, with special and esoteric ties to the CIA".

The article goes on to say that persons close to Angleton have confirmed this account in recent interviews. Reflecting Mr Angleton's own position, however, they have denied assertions from other sources that the CIA team made fissionable material — plutonium — available to the Israelis from United States stocks.

Mr Szulc asserts that "Angleton's firing was related to the preeminent role he played in the relations between the CIA and Israeli intelligence, something which both Secretary of State Henry Kissinger and Colby had resented for a long time. The domestic spying controversy was a convenient excuse for doing away with Angleton and his strongly pro-Israeli personal views.

The *Penthouse* article is one of a series on the role of the United States intelligence agencies. It also discloses that the CIA attempted to kill President Sukarno of Indonesia in the late 1950's, and that in 1958 the CIA seriously considered the murder of Mr Chou En-lai, the Chinese Prime Minster, during a visit to Rangoon.

The latter plot was never carried forward, but the attempt at Dr Sukarno's life was aborted and "at least one American pilot, employed by the CIA, was captured by Sukarno's forces during the coup attempt."

Mr Szulc explains: "To kill Sukarno the CIA, according to

intelligence sources, planned to fire a shell from a ceremonial 105mm cannon in front of the presidential palace while Sukarno spoke from a balcony. The plan, however, was vetoed at the highest levels in Washington."

Concerning the Chou En-lai assassination plot, Mr Szulc says the setting was to be his visit to Rangoon. "This was at the beginning of the Soviet-Chinese split, and apparently the CIA reasoned that Chou's death would aggravate the developing split."

He continues: "The notion was that Chou was a moderate and thus posed an obstacle to a possible Soviet-Chinese confrontation. Furthermore, intelligence sources said, the CIA planned, by the dissemination of "disinformation" through intelligence channels, to lead the Chinese to believe that Chou was killed by the Russian KGB (secret police)."

Mr Szulc goes on to say: "This murder plot, which was also stopped by Washington, provided for a Burmese CIA agent to place untraceable poison in a rice bowl from which Chou was expected to be eating at a government dinner in his honour."

This particular poison, intelligence sources said, "would have acted within 48 hours and there would be no trace of it if an autopsy were performed. The plan was countermanded at the last moment."*

It is extraordinary that such an article should appear on the front page of *The Times* — without date-line or accreditation and replete with "intelligence sources" and plots that never came off because they were invariably "aborted" — and just at a time when Dr Henry Kissinger was about to start a new round of negotiations between Egypt and Israel. Moreover, I have since learned that the lead time for the publication of *Penthouse* may be the order of two or three months. Why then, one

---

*For another account of this alleged incident see "Armies of Ignorance" by W R Corson (The Dial Press, New York, 1977) pp 365 and 366. He bases his version on the U.S. Senate Select Committee on Intelligence "Foreign and Military Intelligence, Book IV", 94th Congress, 2nd Session, Report No 94–755 (U.S. Government Printing Office, Washington, DC, 1976) p 128. It disagrees with the account in *The Times* by placing the location for the planned assassination of Chou-En lai at the Bandung Conference rather than at Rangoon nearly 2000 miles away; it asserts that the plan was rejected by CIA Headquarters.

might ask, was *The Times* giving such prominence to such stale "news" on this particular day when Kissinger was arriving in Israel, and why was there no accreditation?* Was it perhaps a deliberate plant from one of the Soviet experts on the Middle East in their western propaganda department, possibly my old colleague, H A R Philby? Did MI5 ever notice this strange juxtaposition of the Dimona and Kissinger stories, or seek a reason for it?

I might make a few further observations. The summer of 1975 seems to mark the first entrance on stage of that nebulous character, one "of several nuclear scientists . . . the most important of them . . . a British-born physicist, now an American citizen working for the United States Government in Washington, with special and esoteric ties with the CIA." Nuclear weapons are at best a touchy subject and if Philby did wish to sow discord between the United States and Israel at that time he could not do better than to hint at possible clandestine help from the former to the latter to evade the terms of the U.S. sponsored Nonproliferation Treaty. To embellish the plot with the proper trappings of science the source refers to "several nuclear scientists" but only points a more definite finger at one, a "British-born physicist now an American citizen". If that source were indeed Philby, he may well have had his 1949 to 1951 colleague in atomic energy at the British Embassy in Washington in mind. However, whoever may have been the prototype of this nuclear physicist, the author of a recent book seems to have been guilty of plagiarism in not acknowledging that he had already been brought on stage in the August 1975 edition of *The Times*, or possibly earlier in *Penthouse*. Some time later, after further disturbing developments, I referred this matter to my own particular "confidential anonymous friends" and was informed that I had definitely been "fingered"!

To the best of my recollection, however, I did not see *The Times*' article until some time after 15 October 1975, on which date I was phoned by Mr Nicholas Horrock, a reporter on the staff of *The New York Times*, who said that he wished to come out to NBS in order to interview me about the Israeli atomic-bomb capability. We set up a tentative date for a few days thence, although I did point out to him that

---

* The adjoining column is credited to "Fred Emery Washington August 20".

I had not been associated with such matters for a great many years — in fact for nearly a quarter of a century! After speaking with Mr Horrock I telephoned the Bureau Legal Advisor who informed me that, if my personal opinion was being sought, any interview should take place at my home and not on U.S. government property.

Our calendar notes are a little confused as to what was said on exactly which day, but it appears that as Mr Horrock had not phoned back by Tuesday, 21 October to confirm the tentative date, our secretary called him to ask if he still wished to interview me as my calendar was already quite full for the rest of that week. He told her that the article had already been held up as a courtesy to me, pending his visit, and could not be further delayed. He went on to say, however, that the article did not involve me as the principal party and that the details could be discussed by telephone; he was at that moment busy with copy, but if I could phone later he would be in the office until 6 o'clock. He also mentioned that before using a name in print they liked to clear the subject matter with the person involved because of the legal aspects.

Accordingly I called Mr Horrock back at around 5.30 pm and told him that if the subject matter of the proposed interview did not relate to Bureau interests I had been advised to meet him at my home or elsewhere "off-site" as might be convenient. He said that his inquiry related to a close British friend of James Angleton who between 1966 and 1969 may have facilitated the transfer of fissionable material to Israel. He asked if I had been called to testify before Senator Frank Church's Select Committee of Intelligence. My name was known to other reporters on Capitol Hill and I was supposed to have taken a substantial quantity of plutonium to Israel around 1968 at President Johnson's request! A denial that any such transfer took place is in fact mentioned in *The Times* article (q.v. p 104). My response was that this was ridiculous, and that no one was going to wander around the world carrying large quantities of fissionable plutonium in a suitcase! In my notes I see that Mr Horrock asked: "Were there any other British friends? As you were educated in England you probably had quite a few".

This more or less terminated the discussion except that I asked him, as I had him on the phone, what had gone wrong recently with the composition in *The New York Times*, as it had become difficult to read some articles because lines and even paragraphs were often randomly interchanged. He told me that this was because they had recently installed a new computer. I commented that I supposed the computer lacked the human compositor's ability to read the finished text, and on that note the conversation ended. To my surprise I did not hear again from Mr Horrock, but I communicated the gist of the discussion to our lawyer Marsha Swiss. Nor was any article on the subject subsequently published.

I did learn later, however, that my name had in fact been given to the Church Committee, and also to Dr Kissinger, apparently in the context of his August mission to the Middle East.

Almost exactly two years were to pass before this matter was to come up again. On Wednesday, 12 October 1977, I was called at home on the phone by a Mr Joseph DeCola, Producer for NBC News, at about 6.45 pm. He asked if he could come to see me "in two or three minutes" about a story he was preparing. I told him that we had not yet had dinner and that I would not be free for at least 30 or 40 minutes. He stated that he would be along in half an hour, but I said not for 40 minutes as I did not wish to get indigestion. I also asked what this story was? He said that he would prefer not to talk about it on the phone. Suspecting that it might again be the Israeli "bomb" business, I telephoned Marsha Swiss and she advised that I could refuse to see Mr DeCola but agreed that I would not then know what it was all about. She told me to be on the alert for tape recorders, I should ask for identification, I should take notes and I should remember that I could not control what was finally published. After the interview I phoned Marsha back and she advised me to complete my notes while they were still fresh in my memory and to advise the NBS Legal Advisor of what had transpired and to inform him that I had already been in touch with Counsel. The following account of the interview with Mr DeCola is extracted from the notes that I made that evening.

He arrived at about 7.45 pm and was accompanied by another man whom he introduced as Tad Szulc. I then immediately realized what was the object of their visit, namely the story that Szulc disseminated about "the British-born physicist" just over two years previously. But there was a new angle, namely the hijacking of the freighter with yellow cake to Israel.

During the one and a half hours that they spent at our house there were two cars parked outside — a large one with two people who sat in the front seat all the time that DeCola and Szulc were with me, and a smaller one in which DeCola and Szulc finally left after Szulc had conversed for a few moments with his two colleagues in the larger car. During the interview Miriam had gone upstairs to iron in front of a bedroom window that overlooked the street. After a while one of the men sitting in the large car got out very unobtrusively, and proceeded on a highly delicate mission into our neighbour's bushes. On leaving and re-entering the car, however, its interior lights came on for a few moments, and Miriam noted that the back seat was packed with television equipment.

Downstairs we had meanwhile settled down in my study and I asked what it was that they wished to see me about. Not wholly unexpectedly, they informed me that they were preparing a special television programme on the proliferation of atomic weapons to Israel and that they had information that had been confirmed that I had been involved in the transfer of intelligence to Israel in connection with the Dimona establishment. I responded, as I had done to Nicholas Horrock two years previously, that the story was ridiculous, that I was no longer expert in such matters, that Yugoslavia was the nearest that I had been to Israel, that this could readily be checked by reference to my official and personal passports, and that I had never engaged in any such activity either overtly or covertly. Further, I asked them to tell me what was the "confirmation" that they said they had of my involvement. Szulc mentioned that these activities were carried out on behalf of CIA; and that there was some kind of Israel-Yugoslav connection although Israel and Yugoslavia did not have diplomatic relations.

DeCola said that one item of confirmation that they had was that I had been placed in an "embarrassing and difficult position by past activities" and that this was used to put pressure on me. I asked what other confirmation he might have but he said that he had nothing more. I told him that I was not in any embarrassing or difficult position and intimated that I was not impressed by this "confirmation"!

Szulc then came up with another confirmatory item, namely that when my name surfaced, and apparently also came to the attention of the Church Committee, he, Szulc, in 1975, had gone to see Jim Angleton with whom they knew I had worked, and had asked him if I had been called upon to "perform certain tasks", Jim Angleton had replied "You are not wrong in this", but asked Szulc not to divulge my name. (In view of my liaison work with CIA from December 1948 until April 1951, Jim Angleton's non-committal answer was certainly not incorrect nor was it, I believe, as staggeringly significant as Szulc seemed to think!)

I was also asked if I had been approached by the intelligence service of any other government for information, and I said "Yes" (having my friend "S" in mind!) "Which government?" But I declined to answer that question and said that anyone working in the field of atomic energy could be so approached. "Had I been asked for information or given any?" I said that I found the second part of that question insulting and suggested that they approach the FBI for further information under the Freedom of Information Act; but Szulc said that this would be refused under section 6B(?) of the Act.

DeCola said that they would be grateful for my co-operation, and Szulc suggested that as they had been so frank with me perhaps I could in turn talk frankly to them. At this point, or later, they also said that they did not wish to imply that they did not believe me. I pointed out that the big difference between my being frank with them and their being frank with me, was that I did not intend to publish what they were telling me. (I feel that I almost owe Mr Szulc an apology at this point for now abandoning my good intention!) I also mentioned that I was not much impressed with the "confirmation" of their information (that I had placed myself in a position to be blackmailed, and also that Angleton had allegedly given a double-negative type of "affirmation" to Szulc's question about my having been called upon to "perform certain tasks"). They seemed sensitive to my use of the word "blackmail" and insisted that they had *not* used the word. I agreed with them, but said that it was a useful word with which to summarize what they had said.

At some point in the conversation one of them suggested that my name would not have surfaced if there were not some point to the story. I replied that I had my own theory why that had happened, and that I felt that it had probably been planted through certain channels with the idea of reaching some receptive ear — in this case Szulc's. I asked Szulc if he would care to tell me how he had obtained the story, but he said that he had got it through intelligence-service contacts and intimated again that he had obtained some kind of confirmation for it in the interview with Jim Angleton referred to earlier. They pressed me several times on this point (how my name could have surfaced), Szulc himself asking why should any one want "to take it out on you after so many years?" I replied that I would not give them any information on the matter without permission from the U.S. Government, that it was sensitive information and entirely irrelevant to the question about which they had come to interview me, namely the transfer of scientific information and materials to Israel. They said that they had not mentioned "materials"; this was true, but I said that Horrock had heard some ridiculous story about my carrying plutonium to Israel, although he had not published it. I was also asked if CIA had asked me to undertake any task for them when I was employed by the British Government. I answered "No."

Szulc again asked me if I were not puzzled by all this. I said that I was for two reasons, the first why my name *had* surfaced, although I did have a theory about that, and the second why anyone should think that Israel was not able to build a nuclear bomb when she had so many competent scientists such as those, for example, at the Weizmann Institute — and there was also the background information available in the Smyth Report. I felt that it was an insult to Israel to doubt their competence. There seemed to be some kind of guilt complex — that no one could build nuclear bombs without having obtained, by some means or another, information from this country. Szulc said he had seen my name in connection with the Weizmann Institute; had I not some connection? I said no, apart from routine Bureau correspondence.

There was a further question whether plutonium was more likely to be used in a bomb than uranium, and once again Szulc asked why my name had surfaced and who would want to hurt me after so long? I said that I could give them no information at all on this matter, but that as I had for a time during the war been in charge of the release of British scientific information to allied countries, such as the United States, the Soviet Union, the Polish and Czechoslovak governments in exile, and many others, there could obviously be many old associations. At 9.15 pm I said that I felt we were getting nowhere and Mr DeCola and Mr Szulc departed.

As in the case of Nicholas Horrock, Joseph DeCola and Tad Szulc apparently reviewed their discussion with me and, exercising their good judgement, decided that there was no point in rehashing the 21 August 1975, story of dubious origin in *The Times,* even if it were embellished with the other imaginary escapades of the British born nuclear physicist in diverting enriched uranium, yellow cake and plutonium to Israel.

That then was the unexciting end of this particular episode of the saga. I could not forsee that in two years time the whole story would be brought to life again more publicly, more dramatically.

10

The Curious Climate of Treason

On 28 October 1979 *The Observer*—a respected English Sunday paper—began the serialization of a book by Andrew Boyle, a British journalist, entitled *The Climate of Treason: Five Who Spied for Russia*. The book itself was published a few days later, on 5 November.

Most of my readers will be familiar with the outline of his story, which ran to some length.* Briefly, it centred round the already well-known characters Burgess, Maclean and Philby and the so-called fourth and fifth men (counting from Philby as the third), who were code-named "Maurice" and "Basil" respectively. On 9 November the *New Statesman* identified "Maurice" as Anthony Blunt, and "Basil" as "Dr Wilfred (*sic*) Mann, a modestly obscure physicist."† The *New Statesman*

---

*The page-references throughout this chapter (unless otherwise indicated) are to the original hard-back edition. After the "fourth man" had been officially identified as Blunt, a second edition, "completely revised with exclusive new material", which runs to 574 pages, was published in paper-back (*The Climate of Treason*, revised edition, Coronet Books, Hodder and Stoughton, 1989).

†I sought clarification of the term "modestly obscure" from my friend Professor Philip H Highfill, Jr, President of the Cosmos Club and Professor of English at the George Washington University, and he assured me that it was the opposite of "blatantly obscure".

continued: "Both men, as far as anybody can tell, are wholly innocent."
On 6 November I had been interviewed by a reporter from the *Daily Mail*, another reporter from the same paper having "identified" me through an old AEC friend now living in New England. He had been telephoned by a *Daily Mail* reporter and asked if he could think of a British nuclear physicist who had been in the United States for some period subsequent to World War II and who had been acquainted with the atomic-energy community. He replied that the only British scientist he knew to have been in the United States did not fit the description because, although he was attached to the British Scientific Office, he was not in the atomic-energy programme. When pressed by the reporter he gave my name. The *Daily Mail*, however, withheld publication of their interview with me until 13 November, after my name had been disclosed by the *New Statesman*.

On 13 November I also gave an interview to a reporter from *The Times*, but this was not, as far as I know, published in that paper although part of it appeared in *The Washington Post* on 21 November.

By 15 November trans-Atlantic telephone calls were arriving at my office and at home, and on 16 November the media more or less laid siege to my office and house. On the latter date my car-pool companion Joe Coyne came to pick me up and came into the house. As most of the newsmen who had been waiting since about 7.30 am had gone for breakfast, I asked Joe to leave by the front door in order to engage the one photographer left on guard, and to drive up the street and round the corner, while I left by the back through a neighbour's garden and up his driveway to the next street where I asked Joe to pick me up. The operation was completely successful and as we drove away I said "Well, what happened?" Joe said that as he left the house the photographer asked if he were Dr Mann, and when Joe told him "No" he nevertheless took his picture about fifteen times! I said "Great, Joe, now your picture will be in the papers tomorrow morning as the sixth man helping the fifth man to escape from his own house!" Joe did not, however, appear to be too impressed with my sense of humour. At work, the Bureau information office kindly answered some forty telephone calls on my behalf. At home our younger daughter Janet acted as a very competent Press Secretary, and established quite a *rapport* with many of the reporters.

That afternoon at the suggestion of our lawyer Marsha Swiss we went down to the Department of Commerce for discussions with the General Counsel as a result of which the following press release was made from the Office of the Secretary of Commerce:

> C. L. Haslam, General Counsel of the Department of Commerce, issued the following statement today:
> "Dr. Wilfrid B. Mann has been a longstanding and esteemed employee of the National Bureau of Standards. The Department of Commerce has no question concerning his loyalty to the United States."

It should be emphasized that this statement, issued from the office of the Secretary, spoke for every Department, Agency and Bureau in the Federal Executive, including the CIA and FBI. In this connection Burke Wilkinson, a contributing book reviewer to *The Christian Science Monitor* wrote in the March 1981 issue of *Dossier* that many of Mann's co-workers in the U.S. government came to his defense in a most spirited way.

17 November was a Saturday and the ladies and gentlemen of the largely British news-force took the week-end off. On Monday 19 November the Attorney General, Sir Michael Havers, was asked by Mr Robert Cryer in the House of Commons "if he will refer to the Director of public Prosecutions with a view to prosecution for breaches of the Official Secrets Act the conduct of Dr Wilfred *(sic)* Mann in connection with the defection of Burgess and Maclean?"

The Attorney General replied "No. I have no information relating to the conduct of Dr Wilfrid Mann which would justify my making any such reference to the Director of Public Prosecutions."

In the meantime, after my interviews with reporters from the *Daily Mail* and *The Times,* I was advised against giving any more interviews, largely because without a full press conference it would be impossible to treat all reporters equitably. I also felt that I should await a more forthright and positive statement from the British Government before discussing the case further in public. Indeed, the press releases through the Bureau of Standards did say I was hoping for this, as the British Government was fully aware of the facts. I had no reason to believe that the cautious phraseology of the Attorney-General was intended to imply anything more than what it said. It was a specific and clear answer to a specific parliamentary question. But while many of my friends in the United Kingdom expressed satisfaction that my name had been cleared, others shared my own disappointment that the British Government had not seen fit to go beyond the wording of Mr Cryer's question and give the same positive assurance of my loyalty which I had received from the government of the United States.

The National Bureau of Standards continued to issue occasional statements on my behalf in response to questions by the media. Finally I made my biographical notes available together with a statement that I would be pleased to read and review any article that had *already* been prepared, but I stipulated that it must have been based on a serious effort to research the chronological data. I would not give any interview that was merely designed to obtain raw material for what would possibly be a sensational article.

Two gentlemen, Mr John de St Jorré of *The Observer* and Professor Allen Weinstein, Professor of History at Smith College, prepared such articles and they discussed the contents with me and confirmed the dated entries in my passports. Mr St Jorré and a coauthor whom I did not meet, Mr Peter Deeley, also interviewed, amongst others, my old friends and colleagues W B Lewis, Alexander King and C P Snow, while Professor Weinstein perused all 3201 documents pertaining to the Burgess-Maclean-Philby affair that had been made available by the Freedom of Information Act. Their articles appeared in *The Observer* on 30 December 1979, and *The Washington Post* (on the "op-ed" page) on 25 January 1980. So far as I was concerned there was nothing more to add to the condensed reports in the Press.

In the previous chapter I have explained that I was well aware that I had been of low-key interest to Soviet intelligence for a number of years. Since 1961, soon after "Mr S" came on the scene I had reported all such unofficial contacts to the appropriate United States authorities. I have also, as a scientist, had many pleasant and interesting official contacts with Russian fellow-scientists; in fact, my contacts with "Mr S" were neither dull nor unpleasant. I have always assumed, however, that those on the "unofficial" level with "Mr S", beginning in 1961, arose from my casual association with Guy Burgess and the official connection with

Kim Philby between 1949 and 1951. Then in 1975 came the articles in *Penthouse* and *The Times,* followed by the investigatory activities of Mr Horrock later in the same year and of Mr DeCola and Mr Szulc in 1977. Then the whole matter was reopened by Andrew Boyle in *The Climate of Treason*. Looking back, I cannot help wondering whether there was some pattern behind what had happened. Initially the "Russian connection" seemed to have been aimed at obtaining from me low-grade information about atomic energy. Burgess may even have been trying to do the same kind of thing in an amateurish way when he sought to develop our acquaintance in Washington in 1950. Is it fanciful to see a wider aim emerging in 1975? Is it possible that what happened then was ultimately instigated by Moscow as an attempt to disrupt the contemporary peace mission of Kissinger to the Middle East, by the use of a fictitious scenario that then developed in 1979 into a "revelation" of treachery, already known to the authorities, that could have undermined western intelligence?

This is only supposition on my part. What I am concerned with is to clear my name from the innuendo resurrected by Andrew Boyle. Perhaps, however, it will not be out of place for me to mention briefly the matter of the "fourth man", Anthony Blunt, who was identified as a traitor as the result of the publication of the first edition of his book. I hold no brief whatsoever for Blunt or for any other traitor to his country, but the part played by Andrew Boyle in "unmasking" him is indeed curious.

I am not the only one to query the part played by Boyle in this matter. It was the subject of an article by Stephen Barber in the *Daily Telegraph* of 20 November 1979, from which I take the following quotations:

> Fear that the unmasking of Anthony Blunt as a former Soviet spy recruiter was really serving Moscow's interests, not the West's, was expressed independently yesterday by two former CIA officials, Mr James Angleton and Mr Kermit Roosevelt. ... Mr Angleton, the CIA's ace counter-intelligence chief before his retirement, said:

> The nagging question that continues to cloud the central meaning of this case is whether the confidential arrangements

made by sovereign governments in granting immunity from prosecution in a matter of espionage have not been flagrantly violated. The culprit is of course the leaker. He has in effect jeopardised, and perhaps permanently, the fiduciary relationship which at times is indispensable if we are to contain and neutralise the steady deployment of Soviet agents and assassins now operating in the West.

Mr Angleton paid tribute to the British intelligence services, who, as he put it, 'are richly deserving of acclaim and support for their perseverance and success in this particular and highly complicated case'... As regards allegations in print recently suggesting that Dr Wilfrid B Mann, a former Briton employed by America's National Bureau of Standards, was the 'fifth man', he declared: 'Dr Mann is a friend of long standing, a distinguished scientist whose loyalty is without blemish.'

He added: 'I am grateful that the Department of Commerce has so affirmed because any insinuation to the contrary is false.'

James Angleton's apprehensions were brought out into the open in the debate in the House of Commons on the Blunt affair which took place on 21 November 1979. In his speech the Attorney General, Sir Michael Havers, reaffirmed the general doctrine that permanent anonymity should usually be inherent in the granting of immunity; and towards the end of his speech he stated without qualification that by granting immunity in this particular case the Security Service had achieved a bonus that it would not otherwise have had.

As against this, Boyle states, in the second edition of his book (p 507):

I am happy to have contributed my part by writing the book that led to Blunt's public exposure and by also helping to kill an odious Protection of Information Bill which might have enabled other undetected moles to go on burrowing undisturbed.

This statement seems to miss the point that Blunt's "burrowing" had in fact been stopped very effectively a quarter of a century ago through the quiet tenacity of the British Security Service, which had then secured the bonus of which the Attorney General spoke—presumably an advantage in the field of counter-intelligence which had helped to maintain the overall security of the realm. It is not necessarily in the public interest that every detail of the work of the counter-intelligence services should be made available just because the British public is (to use Boyle's own word) "obsessed" with questions of espionage.

The purpose of this digression is to ask what good purposes has been served by forcing the Government to identify a poor fish (to borrow an analogy from Boyle) that had been played and safely netted so many years before. But before I leave the debate in the Commons I should like to mention one item that gave me considerable pleasure, and that was Mr Callaghan's warning that "innocent names will be bandied about; indeed they have already been bandied about". I was grateful to him. I felt that perhaps he had me and my family in mind.

So much for the Fourth Man—who is at any rate a character of flesh and blood. When we turn to the Fifth Man we are dealing with a much more shadowy figure. He surfaced, without a name, in *Penthouse* and in *The Times* in 1975; he was investigated, as I have already explained, later in the same year and again in 1977 but neither Horrock nor DeCola and Szulc were able to identify him. He reappeared in *The Climate of Treason* in 1979—but this time bearing my own middle name of Basil. After all these years of harassment I freely admit that I must be the intended target of the innuendo. In November 1979 Jim Angleton said to me "There is no question but that 'Basil' is you." And that there may be no uncertainty about what he meant by this, he was not making an *accusation*. Indeed he had already offered to go to the U.K. to testify on my behalf should that be necessary. He was merely drawing a logical *conclusion* from Boyle's text. The same conclusion was drawn by Phillip Knightley* in a review of *The Climate of Treason* which appeared in *The Sunday Times* on 15 June 1980. I quote the following extract:

> And, although Boyle now implies that he knows the names of at least some of the 25 other moles at last week's press conference to launch the paperback version, he named no one.

*Coauthor of *Philby: The Spy who Betrayed a Generation,* by Bruce Page, David Leitch and Phillip Knightley (André Deutsch, London, 1968: Penguin, Harmondsworth, 1969).

Boyle offers two reasons for not doing so. One is that 'It is for the Government, not authors, to name names when the public interest requires it.' The other, far more convincing, is 'for sound legal reasons' that is, the risk of a libel action.

There is little doubt that Boyle would have named Blunt and Dr Wilfrid Mann, a British-born scientist now in the U.S.A., as Soviet agents (an allegation Dr Mann vigorously denies) if he had been able. Since truth would have been a sound defence against any action by Blunt and Mann it is a reasonable assumption that when Boyle published his first edition he lacked legal proof of his allegations.

So he used a sophisticated manoeuvre to avoid possible legal action. He gave Blunt and Mann code names. They became, respectively, 'Maurice' and 'Basil'—Maurice presumably from the homosexual hero of E M Forster's last published novel, and Basil from Dr Mann's second name. Boyle then set about mentioning Blunt in the text as often as possible, even on occasions when there was no real reason for doing so.

Mann's links with the narrative are too tenuous to do this, so he appears under his own name just once, but it is only 19 lines away from a reference to 'Basil', and Mann's name is dragged into the story in an obviously forced manner: he is a guest at a Philby party in Washington who went home by taxi and returned next morning to collect his car.

On this review I would make three minor observations. Andrew Boyle has never made any *direct allegations* about me—neither has he ever, as far as I know, admitted that the connection made by part of the press between me and the "Fifth Man" was without foundation. It is not strictly correct to say that Boyle gave Mann a code name; it was to the "Fifth Man" that he assigned the code name "Basil". And as I have previously explained, I actually returned home from that notorious dinner party in Washington in a friend's car and not in a taxi.

With its main thesis, however, I would not quarrel. And if we accept, for the sake of argument, that "Basil was I"—in the sense that Jim Angleton came to this conclusion—then it is not unreasonable for me to point out that what is said of "Basil" in *The Climate of Treason* just does not fit in with the facts of my life as I have described them in the previous chapters.

Thus, according to Boyle:*

"Basil" entered the scene "not long after the surrender of Japan" in 1945 and "proceeded to complicate the already involved and troubled life of Donald Maclean". He is described as being "a pleasant Englishman of homosexual bent, a gifted physicist some six years older than Maclean and a covert Marxist, who had studied in London, as well as at the feet of one of the western world's leading nuclear physicists and now held several positions of trust as an official coordinator between the teams of scientists engaged in producing the first nuclear bombs[28]."†

"Maclean started to keep the minutes of the Combined Policy Committee on the intricacies of future nuclear development", in which task without "the prompt and systematic supervision of this agreeable self-effacing fellow agent", he would have "floundered hopelessly out of his depth". In this position he was able to obtain "first-hand evidence on arrangements in the United States for stockpiling and controlling both the vital raw materials and the completed weapons". When Maclean's drinking habits drew attention to him, American agents "particularly noticed his association with 'Basil', the English physicist". The "fact that 'Basil' had regular meetings, invariably alone, with the First Secretary of the British Embassy, a person of obvious instability, induced the FBI to redouble its vigilance from late 1947 onwards."

It was James Angleton, however, of the newly fledged CIA who learned from Jewish intelligence agents "the name of the British nuclear scientist whom they had unearthed as an important Soviet agent[44]."‡ For various reasons, the scenario continued, Angleton decided not to share this knowledge with his British colleagues. He

---

*The Climate of Treason: Five Who Spied for Russia, p 195 et seq.
†"28 Confidential information to the author [Boyle] from CIA sources in Washington", ibid, p 464.
‡"44 Confidential information to the author [Boyle] from the same CIA source as note 42. "42 Confidential information from a former CIA official who prefers to remain anonymous", ibid, p 465.

arranged for "Basil" to be "turned". "Basil" agreed to change sides as directed, gratefully accepting guarantees of protection and the promise of American citizenship when his work was done". "Until October 1948 the British scientist continued to see Donald Maclean as regularly as ever, advising him which nuclear-programme files, and which items on those files, should be extracted from the U.S. Atomic Energy Commission's head-quarters whenever the First Secretary used his special unauthor-ized pass to gain entry, unattended. The information thus obtained was carefully monitored by the Americans before 'Basil' handed it to Maclean, for transmission to the Russians. The relationship between the turned British scientist and the unsuspect-ing British diplomat remained harmonious and unruffled until the autumn of 1948."

After Maclean's departure, "Basil's" task was "to keep a vigilant eye on Philby"* and also apparently on Burgess.† After the defection of Burgess and Maclean, and "now that Philby's cover had been effectively 'blown'..." the "former Fifth Man could be stood down at last to enjoy the benefits of American citizenship with his wife and children. A useful, specialised job awaited 'Basil' in Washington. He had earned his reward."‡

These selected quotations present, I think, a fair summary of the description Boyle gives of "Basil" and his activities. This description gives rise, however, to two questions, the one addressed to me, the other to be raised by me. The first is "Are you 'Basil'?" and the second is "Was there ever a Fifth Man such as Boyle's 'Basil'?"

It is true that I am a physicist, and that my middle name is Basil, but I do not accept for myself the attributes, leanings or political attitudes claimed for him. I am in fact rather less than five years older than Maclean. I did study in London, at the Imperial College, and then in Copenhagen (1932–3). Niels Bohr, to whom Boyle is clearly referring as "one of the western world's leading nuclear physicists", was indeed working there, and I have already mentioned my acquaintance with him. But I did not "study at his feet". I went to Copenhagen to work as a

*Ibid, p 346.
†Ibid, p 360.
‡Ibid, p 377.

research student with Martin Knudsen, that grand old experimenter into the kinetic theory of gases.

There are other questionable statements in Boyle's account, as quoted above, which are perhaps of peripheral importance and call for brief comment only: among them is the question of his "special unauthorised pass". This was neither special nor unauthorized. It came to him by virtue of his office as Secretary of the CPC. It was almost certainly issued by the office of the General Manager of the AEC. It was an official no-escort "permanent pass to the Commissioners' Headquarters" that was *withdrawn* in 1948.* Nor was such a pass to an alien unique. There was for instance another intergovernmental body, the Combined Development Agency (CDA) that was concerned with the exploration for, and the procurement and allocation of, raw materials. Its secretariat in the late 1940s comprised two non-scientist civil servants, one from the U.S. AEC and one from the U.K. Ministry of Supply, the late P J Eaton. During those years that I knew John Eaton (1948–51) his office was in the AEC headquarters and he and his secretary had *no-escort* passes.

More important are specific statements that I can check against the hard facts of date, place, and the context of my own life, as follows:

1. "Basil" now held several positions of trust as an official coordinator between the teams of scientists engaged in producing the first nuclear bomb

As I recounted in Chapter 2, I was a member of the original M.A.U.D. Technical Committee, but I withdrew from this work in 1941 because I did not believe that it would be of any avail in the struggle against Nazi Germany.

According to *Statements Relating to the Atomic Bomb,* published by His Majesty's Stationery Office in 1945, Sir James Chadwick was *the* official scientific coordinator. Thus it is stated on p 23 of this document:

(g) *Transfer of British TA Research Groups to U.S.A.*
86. In August 1943 Sir John Anderson visited America and discussed with the U.S. authorities the means by which the cooperation between the two countries might best be placed on a

Ibid, pp 297, 298.

more formal basis. Further discussions took place subsequently between President Roosevelt and Mr Churchill which led to the setting up of a Combined Policy Committee in Washington.

87. Professor Sir James Chadwick who was appointed Scientific Advisor to the British members of this Committee examined, with those responsible for the scientific and technical direction of the American project, the question whether there were any further steps which could be taken, in the pooling of scientific and technical effort which would accelerate the production of atomic bombs in the U.S.A.

Further reference to this matter is to be found in paragraph 12.23 *of Atomic Energy for Military Purposes* by Henry DeWolf Smyth* and in *Men and Decisions* by Lewis L Strauss†, p 369 *et seq.* The former author mentions that James Chadwick and Niels Bohr spent a great deal of time at Los Alamos where they gave invaluable advice, and that Chadwick was head of British delegation that contributed materially to the success of the laboratory.

Lewis Strauss deals extensively with the Quebec and Hyde Park Agreements. The Quebec Agreement of 1943 was an agreement between the U.S. and the U.K. that set up the Combined Policy Committee (CPC) to make recommendations to the two governments on the objectives of the atomic-energy programme and the allocation of British scientists to U.S. laboratories. Canada was not a signatory to the Quebec Agreement, but, as a partner in the atomic-energy programme was represented on the CPC by C D Howe, its Minister of Munitions and Supplies.

The Hyde Park Agreement was signed by President Roosevelt and Prime Minister Churchill at Hyde Park in 1944 and provided for U.S.-U.K. co-operation in developing atomic energy for military and commercial purposes *after* the defeat of Japan. It was, however, as Lewis Strauss points out, "effectively breached by the McMahon Act" in 1946.

---

*Maple Press, York, Pennsylvania, 1945.
†Doubleday and Company, Inc, New York, 1962.

Both agreements, which had never been presented to the U.S. Senate for ratification, were replaced in 1947 by a *modus vivendi*, also known as the Blair House Agreement that permitted the exchange of information in nine areas, excluding that of weapons.

Alexander King is also quoted in *The Observer*, 30 December 1979, article by John de St Jorré and Peter Deeley as saying that Chadwick had an office in the Dupont Circle Building with the British Commonwealth Scientific Office (BCSO). I have mentioned earlier that I occasionally met Chadwick at that time.

There was no other official coordinator. His only staff in his BCSO office was secretarial, its principal function being to channel information and to provide assistance for British scientists travelling to and from Los Alamos, where he himself was a frequent visitor.

I have described in Chapter 3 above the work that I myself was doing in the years 1943 to 1945 when I was in Washington. My activities were in fields other than atomic energy; this fact is mentioned in *The Observer* article (see p 136) and is documented in the various communications appended to this book.

2. Maclean was able to obtain information on arrangements for stockpiling atomic weapons

The CPC continued after the enactment of the Atomic Energy Act, but, as indicated above, any release of information to aliens on nuclear weapons, or for that matter to unauthorized Americans, was strictly prohibited. Maclean could not therefore have received such information simply by virtue of his position as U.K. secretary to the CPC. After the passage of the Act CPC functions were limited to general policy matters for the consideration of which any of the three governments could request a meeting; it did not meet regularly. This question is considered more fully on p 130.

3. "Basil" advises the First Secretary which items to extract from designated nuclear-programme files. "The information so obtained was carefully monitored by the Americans before 'Basil' handed it to Maclean, for transmission to the Russians"

This is, to say the least, an implausible procedure. Maclean was told which specific items to extract from the files and although he had microfilm equipment of his own,* he apparently gave these items to "Basil" who then handed them back to Maclean; and the latter was unaware that they had been "monitored" and presumably doctored. Was Maclean that stupid? It might have been more plausible to have placed the doctored items themselves in the specific files to be left open that night (in spite of the double-checking at the end of the day and checks through the night by the security guards—or perhaps with their collusion and with whole drawers filled with doctored documents?).

4. The relationship between Maclean and "Basil" continued until October 1948

I, on the other hand, returned to the United Kingdom in the Autumn of 1945. So did Sir James Chadwick, in order to resume his Chair of Physics at the University of Liverpool.† I myself taught for the academic year 1945–6 at the Imperial College in London. When I did cross the Atlantic again in July 1946, it was to Canada to take up a position in the atomic-energy project at Chalk River. In the course of my two and a half years in Canada I spent a few days in Ann Arbor, Michigan, at the end of July 1946, and then between 15 August and 22 December 1946 I was eight or nine weeks in New York and Lake Success with the U.K. Delegation to the United Nations.

In the remaining two years until we returned to Washington on 21 December 1948, I returned briefly to New York on official business in January and August 1947, and spent a week-end touring with friends in upper New York State in October of the same year. Then in April/May 1948 we spent about ten days at the American Physical Society meeting in Washington and visiting friends in Princeton on our way back to Canada. All of these visits I have meticulously recorded in Chapter 4. My movements throughout the five years 1943 to 1948 could easily have been checked through the British Embassy in Washington and through

*_Ibid,_ p 291.
†Letter of 2 March 1947, from Sir James Chadwick to W B Mann, p 155 in Appendix A.

the records of the Imperial College, the United Kingdom Ministries of Production and Supply and the Atomic Energy Authority.

5. *After the defection of Burgess and Maclean and consequent "uncovering of Philby" the former "Fifth Man could be stood down to enjoy the benefits of American citizenship with his wife and children. A useful specialised job awaited 'Basil' in Washington"*

Burgess and Maclean defected on 25 May 1951. My family and I sailed on the *Britannic* from New York for Liverpool on 18 April 1951. I did not return to Washington until 11 December 1951. I became an American citizen in 1959.

More generally, let us summarize the brief career of "Basil", as Boyle sees it, and compare it with the details of my own activities over the same period. According to Boyle:

Basil entered the scene in late 1945.
The "Basil"-Maclean relationship continued "until 1948".
"Basil" confessed "to the Americans in 1948"*
Burgess and Maclean defected in May 1951 and "Basil" was "stood down" soon after.

There is nothing to indicate that "Basil" left Washington during this period from late 1945 to mid-1951, either in his initial period with Maclean under Soviet control, or subsequently when he was under CIA control as a double agent. I, on the other hand, made eleven one-way trans-Atlantic trips in the same period. Apart from two short official visits to London headquarters in May 1949 and August 1950, that I have not mentioned, these usually involved extended sojourns in England, Canada or the United States. In those six years I spent a total of more than a year in England, and about two years in Canada. As eight of these trans-Atlantic crossings were by ship I also spent a total of about two months mid-Atlantic! We left the United States on 18 April 1951, more

Ibid. p 22.

than a month *before* Burgess and Maclean defected, for the United Kingdom where I was to take up a position in the U.K. Atomic Energy Authority with access to all aspects of its programmes. The "Admiral" in a letter dated 18 May 1950 had offered me a further year in Washington as his representative in the field of atomic-energy intelligence. As the correspondence reveals, it was entirely my choice to return home. "Basil" confessed "to the Americans in 1948." Apart from a few days in April/May, I spent the whole of 1948 (until we returned to Washington on 21 December) in Canada and the United Kingdom. In that period, however, "Basil" advised Maclean "as regularly as ever", returning information to him "that was carefully monitored by the Americans".*

There is little more that can be said in reply to the first question raised on p 122, "Are you 'Basil'?"

My activities and whereabouts during the years from 1945 to 1951 can be corroborated by means of the appended letters and other references,† which represent, however, only a small but important fraction of the papers that I have on my files covering that period. As a scientist trained in the practice of logical deduction it would seem to me that "No" is the answer to the first question.

Then there is the second question, "Did Boyle's 'Basil' ever even exist?" And let us not forget that Boyle did not create "Basil". "Basil"

---

*Ibid, p 311.
†Photocopies of these documents have been made available to Mr Robert Maxwell, Publisher of Pergamon Press, as have also my passports to Mr John de St Jorré (*The Observer,* 30 December 1979), and Professor Allen Weinstein (*The Washington Post,* 25 January 1980). Reference can also be made to various papers, articles and talks that I authored, edited, co-authored or gave from 1946 to 1949, namely *Reports in Progress in Physics,* Vols VIII, IX and X (The Physical Society, London); The Royal Society Empire Scientific Conference, 20 June 1946; "The Imperial College High-Voltage Generator" by W B Mann and L G Grimmett in Vol 59, 699, of the *Proceedings of the Physical Society* (London, 1947); United Nations Report on "Scientific and Technical Aspects of the Control of Atomic Energy"; Canadian Association of Professional Physicists, London, Ontario, 12–14 June 1947; *The Physical Review,* 15 September 1948; National Research Council of Canada Reports CRM 408, 409, 410 and 411, September 1948; *Review of Scientific Instruments,* January, 1949; and two papers in the *Canadian Journal of Research,* Section B, June 1949. The first referenced paper, with L G Grimmett, actually gives a rather complete chronology of my association with that project from 1939 until October 1946.

made his début, courtesy of *Penthouse* and *The Times,* in 1975. Boyle merely code-named him and tried to give him a little more substance.

My tour of duty at the British Embassy in Washington was from December 1948 (nearly three months after Maclean, whom I never met, had returned to the United Kingdom) until April 1951. For some part of that time I was working under the same Chancery roof as Burgess and Philby. I have dealt in some detail, in Chapter 6, with my relationship with each of them. The fact that I never came across any other British scientist remotely resembling "Basil" and working in the same milieu lends much credence to my assumption that he did not exist.

I do not wish to labour the point but there are still many people who can confirm that I was the *only* scientist at the British Embassy with a background in nuclear physics. On the other hand, I can find no specific reference in *The Climate of Treason* to the British ministry in the U.K., or office in Washington, with which "Basil" was connected. He was merely an "official coordinator", and one is left with the vague impression that he might have been attached to the British Embassy, or have been a very frequent visitor who "held regular meetings, invariably alone, with the First Secretary [Maclean]"* Nor have any friends of "Basil" seen fit to approach me since Boyle's book appeared in 1979, although one could suppose that he might have had some in Washington.

Sir Roger Makins was the Minister whose responsibilities embraced "most significantly the problems of atomic development".† No British official, especially after the advent of the Atomic Energy Act, could operate footloose and fancy free even on the fringes of that field at that time in Washington without some kind of official accreditation. "Basil" *must* have reported to Makins if he was *officially* concerned with nuclear-energy matters; or later to Sir Frederick Hoyer Millar who took over responsibility for such matters from Makins, and was the Minister to whom I reported. I did occasionally see Sir Derek at work, and Miriam and I also visited his home. Under such circumstances it seems inconceivable that I could avoid meeting "Basil" either at work or at any of the Embassy social gatherings—especially if "Basil" had been such a

*_Ibid,_ p 305.
†_Ibid,_ p 295.

close associate of the sometime "acting Head of Chancery",* Donald Maclean, until only three months before our arrival in Washington! Neither I nor anyone I knew ever met this "Basil"—this apocryphal "distinguished British nuclear physicist".†

Although, as I have pointed out in my Preface, non-evidence is no evidence, I find it very hard to believe that in the friendly, highly social, diplomatic circle in Washington that we should not have heard about "Basil". At the British Embassy itself I gave a farewell talk on "Atomic Energy" and was later told that I was known to the Embassy staff as the "atom bomb." Is it conceivable that no one would say anything to me about "Basil"? I cannot *prove* that "Basil" did not exist—but I am pretty sure that he did not!

There are, however, two further reflections: Firstly, would Jim Angleton have allowed a turned-around "Basil" access to the high-security precincts of CIA to persue decoded intercepts, as I was in 1949, 1950 and early 1951? Knowing Jim pretty well, I would say that would have been impossible.

Secondly, one has to evaluate Maclean's likelihood of obtaining vital information relating to nuclear physics from the files at the Atomic Energy Commission Headquarters. His position was that of U.K. secretary to the Combined Policy Committee that had been set up at the time of the Quebec Conference to coordinate the "scientific and technical effort" towards the production of nuclear bombs (see p 124), and comprised representatives from all three of the so-called tripartite countries—Canada, the U.K. and the U.S.A. The McMahon Atomic Energy Act, signed into law by President Truman on 1 August 1946, prohibited the export of classified technical information on the development of nuclear energy and thus reduced the function of the CPC to a shadow of its war-time importance. It was now concerned with such policy matters as might arise at a high governmental level, but mainly with respect to the availability and sharing of raw-material resources, and with the economics and politics of international cooperation, matters that were well within the scope of Maclean's professional competence. By virtue of his position at the

*Ibid, p 300.
†Ibid, p 304.

British Embassy, Maclean was presumably privy to exchanges between Prime Minister Attlee and President Truman on questions of atomic-energy policy, and also to our less confidential thoughts on the international control of atomic energy expressed in communications home from the U.K. delegation to the United Nations. But the idea of his wandering around AEC Headquarters after hours, poking into files on nuclear physics under the remote guidance of "Basil", and finding worth-while information without even any knowledge of the filing system, to me is incredible. AEC security required that all files be locked, double-checked by the security guards at closing time, and rechecked regularly throughout the night, and not left open for casual inspection by any prowling predator during the night. Lewis Strauss has written* that "The Commission adopted many of the procedures of the Army's Manhattan District, among which was the wearing of badges in security areas." It was in fact one of the most carefully designed security systems in existence at that time and was continually being subjected to scrutiny. Although some lapses of security are always possible in the best of organizations, just the right AEC filing cabinets were not going to be left unlocked, night after night, for Maclean's leisurely inspection.

Little remains to be said about these events that took place more than thirty years ago and that have almost passed into early twentieth-century history. But quotations from a couple of newspaper articles may still be of interest. The first appeared in *The Washington Post,* written by James Lemoyne and Leonard Downie, Jr, with the dateline "LONDON, Nov 15" (1979). It quotes Andrew Boyle in part as follows:

> I didn't name Blunt in my book' Boyle said in an interview tonight. 'It wasn't my job. It's for the government to say these things. I'm not in the business of doing its dirty work.'
>
>   I'm a Christian and I think this is fair,' he added when asked his feelings about Blunt.

The second quotation is from an article written by Andrew Boyle in *The Observer* and reproduced in *The Washington Star* on 18 November 1979. It concludes:

Men and Decisions by Lewis L Strauss, p 256 (Doubleday and Company, Inc, New York, 1962.

Whether the unmasking of Blunt will lead to the disclosure of further names is another matter. I doubt if that will happen. I certainly have no intention of making public what I know, preferring that the authorities should do their own dirty work. [But he is nevertheless 'happy' when he contributes—see p 118 .]

That is why the fifth man, code named 'Basil', will have to wait until the American authorities unmask him—if they ever do. I must at all costs retain my consistency.

My only comment is that if I had real and valid information about a possible breach or lack of security I would bring it to the attention of the proper government authorities, as indeed I felt that I had an obligation to report my concern about Philby to the U.K. and U.S. governments in 1951.

What has happened since the first publication of *The Climate of Treason* is interesting. It created rather less sensation in the United States than it did in the United Kingdom. Indeed, after the first flurry of excitement, engendered mainly by the U.S. representatives of the British press, interest in the matter subsided.

From the start there were those who felt unhappy about Boyle's approach to the question of the Fifth Man. I have already referred to an article by Professor Allen Weinstein that appeared in *The Washington Post* on 25 January 1980 (see p 116). In this article he says that while Andrew Boyle's "confidential" information from what Weinstein calls "informant-spooks" cannot of course be confirmed, his claim to have obtained help from the CIA and FBI files made available by the Freedom of Information Act* should be verifiable. But the CIA release consisted of only five documents, none of which contained new information. The FBI had no less than 3196 pages of material on the case. These had been available for researchers for a long time. Most of them were newspaper cuttings or reports of parliamentary debates. The rest covered the somewhat haphazard investigation which the FBI carried out into the activities of Burgess, Maclean and Philby while they were in America, but *after* they had left.

Weinstein pointed out that Boyle had attached considerable

*Ibid, p 10.

importance to these documents, the significance of which was stressed by some of those who reviewed his book. Unfortunately it was on evidence of this type that Boyle's "Fifth Man"—"Basil"—was widely identified in the British and American press as "Dr Wilfrid *Basil* Mann".

But Weinstein confirms that I have produced my passport and other records to show that I left the United States in September 1945 and that it was not until late December 1948—months after Maclean left Washington—that I returned. Certainly he did not consider there was anything in the FBI and CIA files to corroborate Boyle's theory.

I quote verbatim the conclusion of his article:

> ... the author [Boyle] told his press conference last week 'I am not in favor of witch hunts.' For that very reason, Boyle might wish to resolve the unsettled matter of the *'fifth'* man' before pursuing publicly further revelations of Numbers 6 through 35. Has Boyle really any cogent evidence identifying the Soviet agent he calls 'Basil' as Dr Wilfrid Basil Mann? If so, he should produce it and counter Dr Mann's denials. If not he might wish to indicate that fact to the journalists who have somehow linked Dr Mann to Boyle's 'Basil'.
>
> Both in Andrew Boyle's England and in this writer's America, there is a serviceable word to describe the activities of the 'fourth man', Anthony Blunt: treason. There is an equally serviceable word to describe *allegations* of treason without cogent evidence: McCarthyism.

More recently, two further books have appeared dealing with different aspects of the Soviet espionage system. One of them, *The Fourth Man,** specifically refers to Boyle's allegations as follows:

> Nor do I entirely absolve the erudite Mr Andrew Boyle from starting hares. ... Whilst correctly identifying Anthony Blunt under the code-name 'Maurice' he also code-named 'Basil' the man who guided Maclean through the intricacies of atomic

The Fourth Man by Douglas Sutherland, p 147 (Martin Secker and Warburg/Arrow Books, London, 1980).

espionage while the latter had access to CIA files *(sic)* in Washington. He afterwards worked for the CIA as a double agent for the next ten years and now, forgiven, lives in happy retirement in the U.S.A. .... *'Basil' may well have existed but he was certainly not Dr Mann, as some newspapers suggested.*(my italics)

Then Chapman Pincher, in his book *Their Trade is Treachery,** states:

Dr Mann, the atomic scientist, who has previously been named, but against whom MI5 has never entertained suspicion ...

and

Dr Mann, the atomic scientist living in the U.S. and recently named as the Fifth Man, and against whom I am assured there is no evidence....

But it was an article in the *New Statesman* of 27 March 1981, which provided the most ironic twist of all. In making some amends for its identification of me—"a modestly obscure scientist" in its issue of 9 November 1979 (see p 113)—it now more recently states that I "successfully repudiated the allegation." But it also mentions the point of view that James Angleton himself was "the main choice for a KGB 'mole'".

The idea that James Angleton, a man of unimpeachable loyalty, could possibly be a "mole" is preposterous. Whose turn will it be next?

This then is the story of how an ordinary scientist was caught up in a web of suspicion. More important than my own experience is the fundamental problem that underlies it. It is a problem which does not and could not arise in the Soviet Union. But we in the western world have to accept that complete security and total democracy are incompatible ideals. Insofar as a degree of democratic freedom exists in

---

Their Trade is Treachery by Chapman Pincher, pp 30, 132 (Sidgwick and Jackson, London, 1981).

our countries, the Soviet intelligence services have scope to operate. If the pack is not to be stacked too heavily in their favour, they must be countered by some surveillance of our own people, and this in itself is an encroachment on freedom. The right balance between the claims of individual freedom and national security is a matter for the government of each country to decide in the light of its own circumstances and traditions, and we must accept that in the process of safeguarding national security *and* our freedom, the innocent cannot always be protected from harassment.

So finally the spectre of the Fifth Man, having served its masters well, can perhaps be laid to rest.

References

[1] *The Cyclotron* by W B Mann, 1st edition 1940, 4th edition enlarged 1953 (Methuen & Co Ltd, London; John Wiley & Sons, Inc, New York).

[2] "The Imperial College High-Voltage Generator" by W B Mann and L G Grimmett, *Proc Phys Soc,* **59,** 699, 1947.

[3] "Ernest Orlando Lawrence, Seventeenth Duddell Medalist", by W B Mann, *Proc Phys Soc,* **53** 1, 1941.

[4] "Professor Leif Tronstad" by Wilfrid B Mann, *Fra Fysikkens Verden,* **27,** 4, 1965.

[5] "Radio Ranging and Nuclear Physics at the Carnegie Institution" by Merle A Tuve, *Facets of Physics,* Ed D Allan Bromley and Vernon W Hughes, Chap 8 (Academic Press, New York and London, 1970).

[6] "Report of The Royal Society Empire Scientific Conference", Vol II, pp 9 and 25 (The Royal Society, London, 1948).

[7] "Scientific and Technical Aspects of the Control of Atomic Energy" (United Nations, Department of Public Information, Late Success, NY, 1948).

Appendix A

Letters Referred to in the Text

University of California
September 9, 1939

Dear Wilfrid,

Under the circumstances it is a very sad business writing you. I never really thought war actually would come, and now it is here. It is evident that many of the plans and dreams of you and I and millions of others are dashed to pieces. We can only hope now that it will be a short war, and that soon the world will return to sanity.

Your good letter and manuscript arrived when I was away on a vacation. I was very sorry to hear of the automobile accident but glad that you both were not seriously injured. Needless to say, it was a surprise to learn that you were over here, and we only regretted that you could not come out to see us. The inscription you suggested is being prepared for the pen on the cyclotron desk.

I read the manuscript with a great deal of pleasure and satisfaction. You have done a first-class job. By the way, the new cyclotron is sixty inches, not fifty inches in diameter. It is very kind of you to invite me to write a foreword, and I intended to do so after going over the manuscript carefully. About the time I finished the manuscript the fall term opened, and I found myself swamped with a succession of unavoidable obligations; and now with the war having broken out, I suppose the book will not be published.

I wonder if you knew that John was on the Athenia. I received a cable from him on last Sunday morning saying that he was sailing on the Athenia, and then about eight o'clock Sunday evening I heard over the radio that the Athenia had been torpedoed and was sinking rapidly. We listened night and day for news of his rescue, and on Tuesday noon the report came that about five hundred had been lost; and not having heard from John, you can imagine my state of anxiety, when about four o'clock in the afternoon he cabled that he was safe and sound in Glasgow. He was picked up by a destroyer.

I do hope that you and Miriam are getting along all right.

Sincerely,
Ernest O Lawrence

———————

University of California
April 5, 1940

Dear Wilfrid,

I feel like a very, very bad boy because it has just dawned on me that I have never written you since receiving the copy of your monograph on the cyclotron. I should have acknowledged it immediately, but I put off writing presumably for a few days until I had read it through, and I took the copy home and put it by my bedside expecting to read it some night, but one thing and another happened, and more than a week passed before I did have the pleasure of reading every chapter. Then somehow or other I slipped up on writing to you, and I hope you will forgive me.

The monograph is excellent in every respect. It is extraordinarily good, and I am sure many people will be glad that you wrote it. We have meanwhile ordered a dozen or so copies, but at the present time the two copies I have here, the one you sent and the one the publishers sent to me, have been in constant use, and everyone is loud in praise of the author. It has been found particularly useful reading for those beginning work in the laboratory. Recently it has been read by such people as President Karl Compton of the Massachusetts Institute of Technology, President Conant of Harvard, and President Bush of the Carnegie Institution; so it is being read by those in high positions as well as beginners.

There is all sorts of news around here, but above all I am glad to report that the Rockefeller Foundation has given us adequate funds to build the 184-inch cyclotron, which will weigh something over 4500 tons. You can well imagine that all of us around here are just now travelling on very thin air as we just got news of this action of the Rockefeller trustees day before yesterday. You can well imagine also that we are going to have our hands full from now on what with the work that we intend to keep going with the 37-inch and 60-inch cyclotrons and at the same time building the great machine.

Well, spring is here, and the war has not taken a serious turn for the worse, and I cannot help but feel that after all the so-called total war will not come off. It seems to me quite possible that neither side will be willing to take the risk of such a catastrophe. Let us hope so anyhow. Meanwhile I hope that everything is going as well as possible under the circumstances for you and Miriam. Molly and I send you our warmest greetings.

> Very cordially,
> Ernest O. Lawrence

> Department of Scientific Research & Experiment,
> ADMIRALTY, S.W.1.
> 11th July, 1940

Dear Mann,

I am very sorry that Imperial College will not let you come to us because I feel quite certain you would have been able to do very valuable work at Swanage. In view, however, of the attitude of your authorities I quite agree that you have no option. I should certainly be very pleased to hear from you if you are free. I do not see any opportunity at the moment of farming out to you any problem for any of the Services. We have of course had similar requests from nearly every University in the country and it is not an easy matter especially at the present time.

Would you let me know the address of J. V. Hughes.

Yours sincerely,
F. Brundrett

———————

Ministry of Aircraft Production,
Millbank, S.W.1.
23rd March, 1941

Dear Sir,

I am instructed to inform you that it has been decided to dissolve the Technical Sub-Committee of the M.A.U.D. Committee and to form in its place the M.A.U.D. Technical Committee under the Chairmanship of Professor G P Thomson with the following terms of reference:—

(i) To consider the problems arising in the Uranium investigation.

(ii) To recommend to the M.A.U.D. Policy Committee the experimental work necessary to establish the technical possibilities.

(iii) To ensure co-operation between the various groups of investigators.

The proposed Membership of the Committee is as follows:—

Professor G P Thomson   Chairman
D.S.R. M.A.P. or representative
Professor P M S Blackett
Professor J Chadwick
Professor J D Cockcroft
Professor C D Ellis
Professor W N Haworth

Professor N F Mott
Professor M L Oliphant
Professor R Peierls
Professor F Simon
Dr M Blackman
Dr E Bretscher
Dr N Feather
Dr O R Frisch
Dr H H Halban
Dr C H Johnson
Dr L Kowarski
Dr W B Mann
Dr P B Moon
Dr B G Dickins   Secretary

I am instructed to say that the Director of Scientific Research will be glad to hear if you are prepared to serve on this Committee. ...

It is notified for information that the Policy Committee will consist of one representative from each of the Universities at which work is on progress and that the terms of reference are as follows:—

(i)   To supervise, on behalf of the Director of Scientific Research, Ministry of Aircraft Production, an investigation into the possibilities of Uranium as contributing to the war effort.

(ii) To consider the recommendations of the Technical Committee and to advise the Director of Scientific Research accordingly.

Yours faithfully,
B G Dickins for Director of
Scientific Research

University of California
March 2, 1942

Dear Wilfrid,

This is a devil of a long time to delay replying to your letter of several months ago which I and Don and others enjoyed ever so much.

I have been hearing about you through G P Thomson, whom I see occasionally for brief moments these days, and I gather, that you are prospering as best could be expected under the circumstances.

My health has been exceptionally good this year, no doubt in large measure due to the effects of the thorough job you did in proposing my health last December? I am sure you put it on very thick. You might have been nervous under the circumstances, but I know that I would have blushed very much. Nevertheless, I must confess that I got quite a kick out of the version in the Physical Society Proceedings.

Our work here now is mostly in connection with the war effort, and therefore, it is not appropriate to describe what is going on, but you can well imagine that we are all very busy and, indeed, under the circumstances of war, feel very fortunate that we are asked to do things of a scientific character. I only hope that our efforts will mean something tangible in the war effort and not prove to be completely fruitless.

Molly and I send you and Miriam our very warmest greetings and good wishes, and we do look forward to seeing you over here again at the end of the war.

As ever,
Ernest O Lawrence

Ministry of Aircraft Production,
Millbank, S.W.1.
22nd December, 1941

SECRET [declassified]

Dear Dr Mann,

The report of the M.A.U.D. Committees has been examined by the Defence Services Panel of the War Cabinet Advisory Committee, which, in turn, has reported to the Lord President.

The decision taken is that the possible fields of application of this new process are so far reaching that developments should remain in the hands of the Government, and that control of the project should be entrusted to the Department of Scientific and Industrial Research.

Inasmuch as the completion of the examination of this project by your Committee, and the acceptance, in the main, of your recommendations, move the whole matter to the stage where large scale experiment and possible production are now our principal concern, a new organisation has been set up on this basis, and I think that the time has come to wind up the M.A.U.D. Committees.

In doing so I would like to take this opportunity of thanking you for the time and thought which every member must have devoted to this very difficult problem, in preparing, in such a short time, so clear and concise a summary of the whole question.

Although the Committees are now disbanded I am sure that the new organisation under D.S.I.R. can rely upon your co-operation at any time when they may want your help or advice.

Yours sincerely,
J T C Moore-Brabazon

February, 2nd 1944

Dear Dr Mann and family!

I have to thank you very much for your Christmas Greetings, which I received today. I am also very grateful for your kind interest with regard to the future of our country.

Things are not too bright in Norway just now; food, clothing, fuel, and almost everything that previously made life worth living is extremely short. Heavy footwear for the winter conditions is a serious question. Children often have to stay inside for that reason. But the people has gathered strength in other ways and I think that Norway will survive after all!

Things are not moving quite so well or quickly since you left us, but still we have no reason for complaints. Several of our mutual friends called for are now here and waiting for their jobs. As usual some departments are working very thoroughly and consequently not too fast. But still the situation as a whole looks rather bright here, brighter than any time before as far as I can understand.

You mention some stamps. Mr H. says that they have been sent to you long ago, but probably lost on the way. (In the Min. of Supply?) They will try to send you a new collection.

The two enclosed cards to The Randers' and Mrs Loechen have been handed over.

I am looking forward to seeing you again next spring but I take the opportunity to wish you and your family the very best of luck for the time to come.

Halvorsen, Fürst, Dahl and Miss Vold ask me to send their best regards.

I hope you enjoy your work and that you have found what you expected. We are still doing our best, which of course is not very much, but are longing for our real home more than ever.

Yours sincerely,
L Tronstad

3rd March, 1943

Dear Mr Dommett,

Very many thanks for your letter of the 15th February in which you ask for my views, from an academic angle, on the question of the employment of scientists for the benefit of the Country after the war.

As I have already mentioned to you I feel that one of the big problems after the war will be the assimilation of the very great number of radio physicists and radio technicians who are being turned out by our Universities and Technical Institutions at the present time, and who are finding employment in Government laboratories and in the armed services. I feel that it will be necessary for some Government-sponsored scheme whereby these men will be enabled to take one year refresher courses in the Universities with a view to gaining knowledge and experience in other fields of physics, chemistry and allied sciences than that in which they are at present experienced, viz. radio. It is true that a great many of these men will be required for the many applications of radio location to navigation, both at sea and in the air, which will arise after the war, but I very much doubt whether this will absorb anything but a very small fraction of the total number at present engaged on such work.

It has also been suggested that science personnel might usefully be employed in some sort of central industrial laboratory which would be available to undertake research work on behalf of small firms and industrial undertakings of insufficient size or importance to belong to one of the larger research associations. There must surely be many small firms in this Country who would greatly benefit from the facilities offered by such a central organization to whom they could submit their technical problems for solution.

I might also suggest that in view of the likelihood of a shortage of scientific equipment after the war, that equipment in Government establishments in so far as it is no longer required, might be disposed of free to the research laboratories of Universities!

> With kind regards,
> Yours sincerely,
> W B Mann

W E Dommett, Esq.
Assistant Director of Scientific Research,
Ministry of Supply

> Privy Council Office
> Whitehall, S.W.1.
> 21 April 1943

My dear Hill,

I brought the question of technical books, raised in Mann's letter, up at the meeting of the Technical Personnel Committee this morning.

It transpired that the Board of Trade already have a Committee about books and the representative of the Board of Trade on my Committee undertook to see that the question was not overlooked at that investigation.

It is possible that either the Committee or the Parliamentary Under Secretary of the Board of Trade may get in touch with you about it.

In the meantime I will keep an eye on it.

Yours ever
HANKEY

Professor A. V. Hill, F.R.S., M.P.,
The Royal Society,
Burlington House, W.1

———

Shell Mex House
London, W.C.2.
24th May, 1943

Dear Dr Mann

The personal chat, in which Professor Linstead participated, which we had on the 19th was, I feel, very useful. The position was discussed and it was left to you to give the matter a final thought. Linstead saw you again and conveyed your wish to me.

Much as I shall regret your severance from our Liaison Section, it is clear that you must have a rest and change and, so, with the greatest reluctance, I must be content to accept your resignation. I understand that, to meet our difficulty you have agreed to allow that resignation to become operative on June 30th, instead of May 31st, as suggested originally and I appreciate very much that extension. I will now put your resignation through to D.D.T.A. for official action.

As you know, it has been decided to send additional physicists to B.C.S.O. and you mentioned this matter during our chat. There is no doubt that you could very usefully employ your liaison experience and contacts while the change should be beneficial to your health. I am, therefore, writing to Sir Edward Appleton suggesting that he approaches you with regard to a post at Washington.

I cannot close this letter without again expressing my deep appreciation of the services you have rendered to the Ministry.

Good luck and best wishes,

Yours sincerely
H. J. GOUGH

24th May, 1943

Dear Appleton,
   Additional Physicist for B.C.S.O.

Arising from the recent decision of the War Cabinet Scientific Sub-Committee, I am dropping you a line about our Dr. Mann. There is no doubt that the arduous work he has been doing for us in the liaison field, combined with his college duties, has resulted in a state of overwork which, if continued, is likely to affect seriously his health. He wishes to resign. I have had a long chat with him and, with very great regret, must conclude that a change is essential in his own interests: we shall, of course, miss him very much, for he is a skilled and most devoted worker. We have agreed that his services with this Ministry shall terminate on June 30th.

In my chat with Mann, the possibility of a post at Washington was raised by him and this has coincided with the need for an additional physicist at B.C.S.O. I am, therefore, writing to you to suggest that you approach him on the matter. I feel the change of work, air and scenery are likely to be most beneficial to his health, while as to the valuable addition to its scientific strength which B.C.S.O. would acquire there is, of course, no doubt.

I have told Mann that I am writing to you on this matter. I now put the suggestion to you to consider and, if you agree with it, to approach him direct, as the B.C.S.O. matter was left to you to handle. You will remember that you wrote to me earlier in the year on this very subject but, at that time, it was not possible for us to release him.

Yours sincerely

H. J. GOUGH

Department of Scientific & Industrial Research

Teddington, Middlesex

27th May, 1943

Dear Mann,

I hear from Gough that you are leaving the Ministry of Supply and following discussion at a meeting of the Scientific Sub-Committee of the North American Supply Committee, I should like to ask you whether you would be willing that I should suggest your name at the next meeting of the Sub-Committee for a post as Physicist at the British Central Scientific Office at Washington. I should be glad to discuss details with you at any time but I should like to have your general reactions to the suggestion in time for the next meeting of the Sub-Committee on Wednesday morning.

Yours sincerely

E. V. Appleton

Shell Mex House

London, W.C.2.

1st July, 1943

My dear Dr Mann,

Your very cordial letter has indeed given me very great pleasure and I do hope that I shall have a chance of a few words with you in the near future; I am sorry that I was away yesterday when you called.

You may be assured that we shall be most pleased to have you again officially associated with us should your other engagements — such as

B.C.S.O. and college work — permit, and I hope that you will keep in the very closest touch with us by letter and by personal contact whenever possible. Needless to say, anything you can do while at Washington in connection with following up matters arising from the visit of Colonel Skinner, or any similar matter, will be most appreciated by us.

I am very glad to have the copy of your book which you kindly presented to me which, apart from its scientific value I shall always keep as a very treasured personal memento of a valued friendship.

With kindest regards,

Yours sincerely,
H. J. GOUGH

Office of the Scientific Advisers,
Ministry of Production,
2, Central Buildings,
Matthew Parker Street
S.W.1.
2nd November, 1945

Dear Cockcroft,

When I saw you recently you kindly offered to mention to Livesey the fact that I might be available for work in connection with your project some time next year and you asked me to write to you to give you some idea of the date when I shall be available. I am afraid, however, that it is not possible to suggest anything more definite than next summer since I would quite like to see the electrostatic generator at the Imperial College on its way to completion before leaving. This might be completed in as little as three or four months, but on the other hand, if materials and labour are difficult to obtain, it may well take a year.

I have told G. P. that I am thinking of making a change, since I have been at Imperial College, off and on, although as a student for the first two years, since 1927. He fully agrees and has suggested that I should try for Aberdeen, but I feel that this would be a move in the wrong direction since I am more interested in the large scale application of radio-active materials which one might be able to do either as a member of your group or possibly at McGill where Collip is also interested in their application to tracer work. There was a vacancy at McGill this summer for which I could have been considered, but I am not clear whether this still exists or not. If it were necessary for me to start work earlier I am sure that the College authorities and Professor Thomson would be most sympathetic to any suggestion; it is just my own wish, if possible, to get the Van de Graaff generator on its way first. I am, however, very anxious to return to the kind of work I was doing with Ernest Lawrence 7 years ago.

I hope that you and your family are keeping well.

With kind regards,

Yours, as ever,
W. B. Mann

National Research Council
Canada
Montreal Laboratory
November 19th, 1945.

Dear Mann,

I was glad to have your letter of November 2nd.

You may know that we have a biological investigation group in this laboratory which is making active preparations for work with the radioactive tracers. It would, therefore, be quite possible for you to join the T.A. organisation and to work on this in the first instance.

The work is at present in the charge of J. S. Mitchell but he is returning to England about mid-December. Dr Mayneord is staying for a further period and we have three good Canadian biologists working here. I will, therefore, suggest to Akers that you should be offered a job in T.A.

If you wish to change from here to McGill at any time, that would be perfectly possible.

Yours sincerely,
J. D. Cockcroft

Applied Physics Laboratory
The Johns Hopkins University
8621 Georgia Ave.
Silver Spring, MD.
May 3, 1946 .

Dear Dr Mann,

It is with great pleasure that we are able to enclose herewith the Naval Ordnance Development Award label emblem, awarded to you by the Chief of the Bureau of Ordnance of the United States Navy for the part you played in the research and development work conducted by this University.

The Johns Hopkins University Applied Physics Laboratory joins with the Bureau of Ordnance in extending to you its congratulations and appreciation for the hearty cooperation and unrelaxed efforts which you so consistently displayed.

Very truly yours,
D. Luke Hopkins
Authorized Representative

Sent: August 9th
Recd: August 10th

COCKCROFT
IMMEDIATE
From HOW

1.   Prime Minister has asked Penney if he can temporarily take over from Sir George Thomson on the Atomic Commission but reply not yet received. Thomson is due to leave New York by air August 13th.

2.   Cadogan and Thomson feel that Mann would be most useful to assist principal U.K. Scientific Advisers on the Atomic Commission, at least during the present period when work on Scientific and Technical side is heavy and continuous. Thomson would appreciate it if Mann could arrive before he leaves i.e. by August 12th. This will be all the more

desirable if Penney is unable to take Thomson's place, in which event there would, in the absence of Mann, be a complete gap in our representation.

3. We should be grateful, therefore, if you could arrange for Mann to proceed to New York on or before August 12th. Departments concerned, including Foreign Office and Cabinet Offices, concur.

High Commissioner's Office, please repeat Immediately to Sir A. Cadogan, U.K. Delegation to United Nations, N.Y.

August 16, 1946

Dear Cockcroft:

Penney was wondering whether any experiments have been carried out in either Canada or the U.K. to detect a possible increase in radioactivity of the atmosphere subsequent to the Bikini test, with a view to discovering whether or not it might be possible to detect the explosion of an atomic bomb. I recollect that the suggestion of such a possibility has been referred to in the press but I am aware of no experiments to test this point ....

There seems to be plenty to do down here; the problem appears to be where to start.

Yours sincerely,
W. B. Mann

31st August, 1946

Sir,

I have the honour to inform you that Mr. W. B. Mann is authorised until further notice to represent me as Scientific Adviser and alternate delegate at meetings of the Atomic Energy Commission and its subsidiary bodies.

> I am Sir,
> Your obedient servant,
> (Signed) ALEXANDER CADOGAN

His Excellency,
Mr Trygve Lie,
Secretary-General of the United Nations,
Lake Success.

> Imperial College
> Imperial Institute Road
> S.W.7
> 16th September 1946

My dear Mann,

I must apologise for not answering your letter sooner, but I have been away, and had to get things fixed up with the Foreign Office on my return. I hope you will be able to spare a few days after my arrival, which should be on the 26th September, but I do not feel that we should be justified in keeping you permanently in view of your commitments at Chalk River. I hope to arrange with the Ministry of Supply for you to be available if necessary. I should, for example, like to have the opportunity of seeing some of the laboratories in the middle west, and if there were a quiet time, I might ask for you to take my place, while on the other hand, if there were a very heavy session both of us might be needed. I hope, if I make this arrangement, it will be agreeable to you.

> Yours very sincerely
> G. P. Thomson

United Kingdom Delegation
to the United Nations,
New York.
Feb. 3 1947

Dear Mann,

I am sorry I didn't see you before your departure. I am afraid you were brought here rather under false pretences, but I am sure you were able to do useful work all the same.

It certainly would be useful if you could give us the result of your reflexions.

Hoping to see you again here.

Yours sincerely
Alexander Cadogan

United Kingdom Delegation
to the United Nations,
61st Floor, Empire State Bldg.,
New York 1, N.Y.
26th November, 1946.

Dear Mann,

I have just heard that you are likely to be coming down on or about the 4th for a day or two. Actually I had planned to write to you this morning to say that I think the 4th is about the date on which you should come to take over from me. I am very much hoping to get a chance of a short holiday and to leave for it on the 6th so that there will be just a nice time to put you "au courant". It is, of course, possible that circumstances may prevent my going, either private ones or the exigencies of the work. In that case, I will wire you, though the only difference it would make, I suppose, would be the amount of clothes you pack. You will by now have got my last letter suggesting that something of the kind was likely.

I now hear that Chadwick will be coming early in the New Year.

Yours very sincerely,
G. P. Thomson

The University of Liverpool
George Holt Physics Laboratories
2nd March, 1947.

Dear Mann,

As I expect you know, Sir Charles Darwin is now in New York with the Atomic Energy Commission, and the intention is that he will be replaced by George Thomson some time towards the end of May. I hope, therefore, that there will be no need to ask you to leave Chalk River again for some time. I explained your position to Cadogan, and he agreed that you should not be called upon to serve in New York unless it was really necessary. I hope you will continue to be kept in touch with developments there, so that you will be familiar with the state of affairs if you should be called upon to go to New York. I do not think that this will be too much of a burden upon your time.

Many thanks for making enquiries about the supply of polonium. I hope that the position will improve. It certainly should not be quite so bad as you point out. There is a quantity of radium D which was sent on loan from Canada to the United States, and I see no reason why Canada should not have first claim on this material. The separation of the polonium is not so difficult to bring the price to 1000 dollars per curie.

I am sending you by separate post a copy of my Melchett Lecture. The reprints arrived while I was in New York, and, although some were sent out in my absence, distribution is not yet complete.

With best regards,
Yours sincerely,
J. Chadwick

The Foreign Office
of the
United States of America

GH:gh
Office of the Military Attache
United States Embassy
Ottawa, Ontario, Canada
8 October 1947

No. C–1182:47
Dr. Wilfrid B. Mann,
National Research Council,
Chalk River Laboratory,
Chalk River, Ontario.

Dear Dr. Mann:

I am happy to inform you that the Department of the Army has approved the award of the Medal of Freedom, with Bronze Palm, in recognition of your meritorious services in the field of scientific research and development during the period of active hostilities in World War II.

If it is agreeable to you, I would like to make arrangements for an investiture ceremony to be conducted by our Manhattan Engineer District representative in Chalk River some time within the new few weeks. If you have any alternate suggestions regarding the manner or place of presentation, please do not hesitate to advise me as I want to have you receive this decoration in the manner you deem best.

Please accept my personal congratulations on winning this high award.

Yours very truly,
R. E. S. WILLIAMSON
Colonel, G.S.C.,
Military Attache.

CITATION FOR THE MEDAL OF FREEDOM
(Bronze Palm)

Doctor Wilfrid B. Mann, United Kingdom, during the period of active hostilities in World War II, performed very meritorious service in the field of scientific research and development. A nuclear physicist who represented in Washington the British Ministry of Supply in connection with research and development of proximity fuzes, he did much to further the exchange of scientific information among British and American groups, contributing substantially to the superiority of Allied military equipment.

———————

Ministry of Supply
Department of Atomic Energy,
Shell Mex House, Strand,
London, W.C.2.
October, 1951

Dear Cockcroft,

Since it was through your kind offices that I joined the Ministry of Supply in 1946 and as, again, you were largely instrumental in getting me the Washington job with [the "Admiral"] in 1948 I feel that I owe it to you to write a few words of explanation regarding my imminent, and somewhat disillusioned, departure from the services of this Ministry. I am also enclosing herewith a copy of my minute of resignation.

First of all I should tell you that I was approached last March by the National Bureau of Standards with a view to accepting an appointment in charge of their radioactivity section. I temporized, however, in the hope that the job Perrin asked me to accept might be one of responsibility and with a reasonable amount of work to do. There has, however, been little to do. This was very disappointing as I had been led to believe (please see the first extract in the annexe to the enclosed minute) that there would be "openings" at the conclusion of my Washington job. In addition [the "Admiral"] has kindly told me that my task in Washington was completed to his satisfaction and in fact that liaison had never been better. You yourself know in what condition I found the job and the difficulties with which I had to contend so will appreciate my disappointment at my subsequent demotion and welcome home!

I have now taken the post at the Bureau of Standards and will there be responsible for the standardization of radioactive isotopes. I shall therefore look forward to continued collaboration with A.E.R.E. and N.R.C. and I hope to pay a visit next week to Harwell to talk to the people there with whom I shall be collaborating indirectly through N.P.L.

It therefore but remains for me to thank you for all your past kindness and interest and to say how much I shall look forward to seeing you in Washington if you have time to spare when you are there. I cannot, however, close without saying how much I have enjoyed the different positions which you have helped me to experience in these last five years; at Chalk River, with interludes at the United Nations, and finally in Washington.

With kindest regards,

Yours very sincerely,
(W. B. Mann)

Atomic Energy Research Establishment
Harwell, Didcot, Berks.
23rd October, 1951

Personal
My dear Mann,

Many thanks for your letter. We shall look forward to having your co-operation on standardisation of radioisotopes in the future.

I am sorry about all the difficulties which have arisen. I think, however, that you are wise in taking the Bureau of Standards job.

Yours sincerely,
J. D. Cockcroft

THE WASHINGTON POST

Letters referred to on page 102.

April 6, 1963

Testing Without Fallout

I have recently read with interest the views of two of your correspondents to the effect that fallout from nuclear tests was bad and that we ought to compromise on the number of inspections.

May I please make a very simple proposition, namely that we take a very strong position in favor of the draft treaty presented at Geneva by the United States delegation on Aug. 27, 1962. This treaty would outlaw atmospheric and underwater tests only and would permit underground testing.

There is very much to be said for underground tests: In general they do not cause fallout, which should satisfy Bertrand Russell; they permit the pursuit of peaceful applications of nuclear energy; they keep in being a team of scientists with experience in nuclear testing (whereas with the abolition of all tests it is impossible for a democracy to keep such a team in existence because free scientists like to test their theories; moreover if, in the event of underground tests being banned, Russia broke an all-inclusive treaty we might be two years behind in assembling a test team again from scratch); it might be possible to obtain the agreement of growing nuclear countries such as France to confine their further testing to underground tests (this limits the size of the device that can be tested but no ambitious non-nuclear country is going to accept the terms of a complete ban which might be agreed upon by the U.S.A. and U.S.S.R.; they might agree to confine their tests underground, however).

WILFRID B. MANN
Chevy Chase.

April 1963

Test-Ban Treaty

I have read the "communication" on the subject of nuclear testing, published on April 9, from a most distinguished group of physicists.

I would like to take issue with them on two points. In the first place a test-ban treaty between the U.S.A. and U.S.S.R. would not necessarily, or in any way, inhibit the urge of non-nuclear powers such as France or China to develop their own nuclear capacity. Secondly we do not require "reasonable assurance that underground testing of small nuclear weapons is not taking place"!

By all means let us permit a limited or unlimited number of such tests! If we do, it removes the need for inspection; they do not cause fallout; they give a reasonable chance for present non-nuclear powers to "sow their oats" and to preserve prestige; they allow experiments in the peaceful development of nuclear energy; underground tests that confine the effects of radioactive fallout are in no different category from tests of biological and chemical weapons that are confined to the laboratory; they keep in being a team of scientists skilled in testing.

Lastly, the banning of just atmospheric and underwater tests is a small step in the direction of general disarmament, and even a small step that reverses a trend is likely to be gratefully accepted by humanity.

This is presumably the purpose of the United States draft treaty proposed on Aug. 27, 1962.

WILFRID B. MANN
Chevy Chase.

Appendix B

Biographical Notes

Date of birth, 4 August 1908. St Paul's School, 1922–7. St Paul's School Leaving Exhibition, 1927. Imperial College of Science and Technology, 1927–30. University of London Scholarship in Physics, 1928. Imperial College Governor's Prize in Physics, 1929. Associateship of the Royal College of Science (ARCS), 1929. Demonstrator, Imperial College, 1929–32. BSc, London, 1930. Diploma of the Imperial College (DIC), 1932. University of London Travelling Studentship, Den Polytekniske Laereanstalt, Copenhagen, 1932–3. Assistant Lecturer, Imperial College, 1933–6. PhD, London, 1934. Commonwealth Fund Fellowship, Radiation Laboratory, Berkeley, California, 1936–8. Lecturer in charge of Third-Year Physics Laboratory, Imperial College, 1938–46. Ministry of Supply, 1941–3. General Editor, *Reports on Progress in Physics,* 1941–6. Physics Society Council, 1942–7. British Commonwealth Scientific Office, Washington DC, 1943–5. Ministry of Supply 1946–51. National Research Council of Canada Atomic Energy Project, Chalk River, Ontario, 1946–8. United Kingdom Delegation to the United Nations Atomic Energy Commission, 1946–51 (Alternate Delegate 1946, Scientific Adviser 1946–51). U.S. Navy Naval Ordnance Development Award, The United States Medal of Freedom with Bronze Palm, 1948. Attache, British Embassy, Washington DC, 1948–51. DSc, London, 1951. Chief, Radioactivity Section, National Bureau of

Standards (NBS), Washington DC, 1951–80. National Academy of Sciences, National Research Council (NAS–NRC) Subcommittee on Beta- and Gamma-Ray Measurements and Standards, 1952–61. International Commission on Radiological Units and Measurements (ICRU), Committee I on Standards and Measurement of Radioactivity for Radiological Use, 1953–62 (Co-Chairman 1953–6, Vice-Chairman 1956–9, Chairman 1959–62). National Council on Radiation Protection and Measurements (NCRP) Committee on Standards and Measurement of Radioactivity for Radiological Use, 1955– (Chairman of Subcommittee M1 1965–6, Chairman of Scientific Committee 18 1966–72, Chairman of Scientific Committee 18A 1972–   ). U.S. Department of Commerce Gold Medal for Exceptional Service, 1958. International Bureau of Weights and Measures (BIPM) *ad hoc* Study Group of the Advisory Committee on Standards of Measurement of Ionizing Radiation, Chairman 1959. U.S. citizen 1959. International Bureau of Weights and Measures, Working Group on Radioactivity, 1960–9. International Bureau of Weights and Measures, Working Group on Radium, 1960–4. Adjunct Professor, Department of Chemistry, American University, Washington DC, 1961–9. NAS–NRC Subcommittee on the Use of Radioactivity Standards, 1962–6. International Commission on Radiological Units and Measurements (ICRU) Planning Board A on Radioactivity, 1964–70. *International Journal of Applied Radiation and Isotopes,* 1965– (Editor 1965–76, Editor-in-Chief for North America 1976–   ). Board of Editorial Advisers, *Radiological Health Data and Reports,* 1966–8. Department of Commerce Representative on the Interdepartmental Committee on Research and Development on Uranium Miners, 1967–9. Federal Radiation Council Working Group, 1967–70. Alternate to the Secretary of Commerce on the Federal Radiation Council, 1969–70. Department of Commerce Representative on the Surgeon-General's Interagency Uranium Mining Radiation Review Group, 1969–71. International Bureau of Weights and Measures, Consultative Committee on Standards of Measurements of Ionizing Radiation (CCEMRI II, Radionuclide Measurements), 1970–   . International Commission on Radiation Units and Measurements (ICRU), Consultant, 1970–   . International Committee for Radionuclide Metrology (ICRM), 1972–   (Vice-Chairman 1975–8, President 1978–80, Executive Board 1980–   ). *International Journal of*

Nuclear Medicine and Biology, Editor, 1973– . Deputy Chief, Applied
Radiation Division, NBS, 1974–6. *Environment International,* Editor,
1977– . National Bureau of Standards Edward Bennett Rosa Award,
1977. United States Senior Executive Service, 1979–80. *Encyclopaedic
Dictionary of Physics in Medicine and Biology,* Editorial Board, 1980– .
NBS Re-employed Annuitant, Senior Scientist, Nuclear Radiation
Division, 1980– . Honorary member, NCRP, 1981. International
Atomic Energy Agency Task Group on Radioactivity-Measurements
Procedures for Secondary Standardizing Laboratories, 1981– .

Index of Personal Names